Will-Developed Intelligence

Will-Developed Intelligence

The Handwork and Practical Arts Curriculum In Waldorf Schools

by

David S. Mitchell

and

Patricia Livingston

Published by:

The Association of Waldorf Schools of North America
Publications Office
3911 Bannister Road
Fair Oaks, CA 95628

Will-Developed Intelligence
The Handbook and Practical Arts Curriculum in Waldorf Schools

Authors: David Mitchell and Patricia Livingston
Photographs: David Mitchell (unless otherwise noted)
Editorial Consultant: Ann Riegel
Proofreader: Nancy Jane
Cover: Hallie Wooten

ISBN # 978-1-888365-19-1
Previous ISBN # 1-888365-19-6

Table of Contents

Part 2

The Waldorf High School

Foreword

The authors, David Mitchell and Patricia Livingston, have over 27 years of classroom experience apiece. They have spent the last two years collaborating on ***Will-Developed Intelligence.*** The book evolved as they shared thoughts on handwork and the practical arts and discussed the wisdom and ideas that lay behind their experiences as teachers. Their gratitude to Dr. Rudolf Steiner deepened with each new insight they discovered.

Even though their expertise is in different areas of the crafts, they made similar observations from their acquired knowledge of the developmental phases of childhood. Each learned from the other in a stimulating and rewarding exchange. The liveliness of their conversations has made this book possible, and they hope that it will be useful to all who read it.

Introduction

by
David Mitchell

The true aim of education is to awaken real powers of perception and judgment in relation to life and living. For only such an awakening can lead to true freedom.
– Rudolf Steiner

During recent years there has been much soul-searching with regard to the aims and direction of modern education in our information-obsessed society. The ancient Greek civilization knew its educational aims. The foundation for all learning was the cultivation of wonder—otherwise, there could be no impulse to explore. In the early years of a child's education, poetry, music, and movement were developed, so that in the student's more mature years, he would have an understanding for mathematics and philosophy. To guide the social life, the religious leaders gave moral instruction through the great dramas written by Euripides, Aeschylus, and Sophocles.

The handwork and practical arts curriculum in the Waldorf school stimulates the creative powers, while at the same time it establishes aesthetic confidence through a conscious guidance of the student's developing *will*. The *will* is the power within us that allows us, through our deeds, to interact with the world. But most importantly, this *will* activity lays the foundation for our thinking.

Biologists have discovered that when we are born, our brain has billions of active neural passageways. These passageways have a correlation with our ability to think when we reach adolescence, if they are correctly exercised during the early and middle childhood years. If they are not used, they simply atrophy. We keep them active through the use of our hands.

The brain discovers what the fingers explore. Our fingertips have a great density of nerve endings. Properly trained, they can discriminate on a level at parity with our eyesight. If our children are not encouraged to be active with their hands, they will become "finger blind," and the rich stimulation through the nerves up to the neural passageways will be diminished.

In the seventeenth century, when the modern scientific outlook was born, education took a new direction. Descartes defined thinking for the Western world. He said that "consciousness is attributed exclusively to the brain and nervous system."

In the twentieth century the educator and philosopher Rudolf Steiner said that if human beings reflect upon the powers of their minds or souls, they will soon discover that they have the capacity of expressing themselves in three different soul worlds—thinking, feeling, and willing. We can experience many different kinds of thinking, from pure logical thought to the rich imaginative pictures of new ideas. The realm of feeling can encompass all heart-related experiences from cultural appreciation to a spiritual experience of ecstasy or devotion. The will life extends from instinctive impulses to conscious deliberate acts. Our educational task is to lead the will from the control of the feeling into the control of the thinking.

In his book ***The Hand: How It Shapes the Brain, Language and Culture***, California neurologist Frank Wilson argues that people who use their hands are privy to a way of knowing about the world inaccessible to those not schooled in manual or practical arts. Speaking on National Public Radio's "All Things Considered," Wilson told of a vice president at a big computer company who complained that his MIT-educated engineers could not solve problems as well as the older engineers at the company. It turned out, Wilson said, that 70 percent of the older engineers fixed their cars, and 20 percent had some experience with wrenches. Of the young hotshots, none had ever held a wrench. As a result, they weren't as good at understanding complex systems.

The hand's knowledge about the world, according to Wilson, actually teaches the brain new tricks. The hand's touching, exploring, and manipulating can reroute the brain's neural circuitry.

Matti Bergström, a professor and neurophysiologist from Sweden, said the following:

> *The density of nerve endings in our fingertips is enormous. Their discrimination is almost as good as that of our eyes. If we don't use our fingers, if in childhood and youth we become "finger-blind," this rich network of nerves is impoverished—which represents a huge loss to the brain and thwarts the individual's all-around development. Such damage may be likened to blindness itself. Perhaps worse, while a blind person may simply not be able to find this or that object, the finger-blind cannot understand its inner meaning and value.*
>
> *If we neglect to develop and train our children's fingers and the creative formbuilding capacity of their hand muscles, then we neglect to develop their understanding of the unity of things; we thwart their aesthetic and creative powers.*
>
> *Those who shaped our age-old traditions always understood this. But today, Western civilization, an information-obsessed society that overvalues science and undervalues true worth, has forgotten it all. We are "value-damaged."*
>
> *The philosophy of our upbringing is science-centered, and our schools are programmed toward that end. . . . These schools have no time for the creative potential of the nimble fingers and hand, and that arrests the all-round development of our children—and of the whole community.*

This book strives to show how the conscious development and training of the hands in the Waldorf currriculum, from kindergarten through the high school, lead through the heart forces to enhanced cognition in students. It also serves as a practical guide to the subjects which make up this curriculum.

Part 1

The Waldorf Elementary School

Photo by Aliki Sapountzi

1

The Importance of Handwork in the Waldorf School

by
Patricia Livingston

Important experiences come about through working with the hands. As teachers, we must help the children become aware of their hands and of the great gifts they bestow on themselves and on others. Their hands need to become skillful, sensitive, and strong, so that they can accomplish many wonderful deeds. Blind people get to know the world through their hands, but most people are unaware of the knowledge that can be gained when they are used in sensitive and useful ways. Think of art and music! Think of what physical work and daily tasks teach us. Think of a handshake and what it tells us about another person.

Handwork and crafts should be imaginatively and artistically taught, encouraging original designs which are colorful and creative in form. The children should learn new ways to use color and make designs that indicate the practical use of the project. Rudolf Steiner gave several indications of how this can be done. The painting and form drawing the children do in all their lessons are extremely important. Working with color and experiencing how colors flow into one another in painting affects everything they do in and beyond handwork lessons, fostering artistic, imaginative growth in their thinking as well.

We want the children to make things they love and enjoy, to work skillfully, always increasing their artistry. Handwork should be relaxing and fun, and at the same time productive, involving strong will activity! Nothing happens if you don't use your hands and get to work! Working to transform the materials of the earth fosters inner growth and a sense of well-being in the children. These lessons support and complement other subjects in the school, helping to bring balance and wholeness to the education.

In the mature artist, handwork and crafts become a balanced activity of thinking, feeling, and willing. The *will* is the part of us that is most asleep. Handwork can gently wake up and educate the will, starting at an early age. Why is this so important?

The *will* is ultimately connected to the thinking. It is really the task of every Waldorf teacher to help the children become clear, imaginative thinkers, human beings who can go into any profession or any area of work with new, creative ideas—ideas that will be urgently needed as we meet the twenty-first century. The whole Waldorf curriculum guides the children in this direction, beginning in the kindergarten, where the creative play of the young child stimulates the inner forces that later become active in the creative thinking of the adult.

Through beauty, color, and form, handwork and crafts help to lead the children from play to imaginative thinking as adults, forming a kind of bridge between the two. The hands play an important part in this awakening. The activity of the fingers stirs the senses that connect the child to the world, and his whole life of thought begins to move.

Handwork and crafts have been taught in all the grades since the beginning of the first Waldorf school. Rudolf Steiner wanted the boys and girls to work together in these classes. In this he was way ahead of his time! It was unheard of to have boys doing handwork in 1919! Why did he insist on this radical change? Because, he said, these activities lead to the enhancement of judgment. Judgment comes out of the imaginative forces, working through the heart. It is not the head alone but the whole human being that forms a judgment. Think how many of the senses are used in handwork—sight, touch, movement, balance, and many others. The senses take in different impressions of the world and join them together to form a judgment. Our hands bring us into a deeper, closer relationship to the world and, therefore, to a greater understanding of humanity.

So much of handwork has to do with waking up, seeing things, and noticing details. Current brain research has found that using the hands opens up neurological pathways that would otherwise atrophy. In other words, the interrelationship of the hand and eye working together allow more neurological pathways to function. So one could say that handwork with young children is a training ground for thinking, and the more one includes the cultivation of beauty and feeling, the more creative will the intellectual thinking become.

Many things are happening simultaneously in the handwork classes. First, of course, one wants the children to learn practical skills, to learn how to use the tools, to respect and care for the tools and other materials involved, and also to form ideas about what they wish to make, creating their own designs, and then actually bringing to completion a beautiful, well-made project. It is a most satisfying experience to make something and see the practical results. This is true confidence building. Therefore, we must see to it that all the projects the children make are things they can learn to do by themselves, that there are no hidden steps done by the teacher, and that the work is finished on time.

Some children need more help and encouragement than others in order to achieve such goals, but the wise teacher will know how to guide them without destroying their confidence and sense of achievement. Confidence in one subject is carried over into another. Activating the will through handwork strengthens ability in all subjects.

There are immense therapeutic possibilities in handwork teaching. Waldorf teachers must study and strive to understand Rudolf Steiner's view of the developing child—an ongoing work for all of us. One must learn to work age-appropriately and study the different types of children—small- and large-headed, etc.—and it is essential to try to understand and work with the temperaments. We must know the children so well that we begin to see exactly what each child needs. How much help will move someone forward? Who needs to slow down and perhaps re-do work that is poorly and thoughtlessly done? How do you handle a melancholic perfectionist? With the older children it is important that they begin to develop some self-awareness in these areas.

Resourcefulness is developed as the children see how much they can achieve starting with a few simple materials. Many simple tasks are no longer experienced in the home. Children today often have no idea how to sew on a button! When a young child learns the "magic trick" of putting a cord in a drawstring bag, he is thrilled! He then becomes more interested and resourceful in solving other problems.

The gifts of nature fill our handwork lessons and create an opportunity to involve the children in the world of ecology and social interaction. The children experience wool, cotton, and many other fibers through using them. They learn of their sources and about natural dyes for colors, and how humanity has contributed to their use. Respect and reverence are fostered for all we receive and for how mankind and nature work together. We should use only natural fibers in our classes, if possible. To touch silk or wool is a very different experience from that of handling synthetic materials. Our Waldorf kindergarten children know that well!

In a first grade, as we use our beautiful wool, we talk about the sheep. If you go to the Rudolf Steiner School in Great Barrington, you probably pass the sheep farm daily. The children see the sheep gradually grow heavy with wool, and then suddenly one day, they see them shorn—a rather shocking experience. So we discuss how generously the sheep give their wool for our scarves and also talk about the craftsmen who spin it into yarn for us. First-grade children know from the fairy tales how "magical" spinning is and still retain a feeling of wonder about spinning straw into gold. We also speak about the trees from which our wooden needles are made. The children learn to value and not waste these gifts. Conversations such as these continue into the upper grades, changing according to the age and to what materials they are using and what crafts they are learning. At the appropriate time modern technology will also be discussed.

All this helps the children make a real connection to their surroundings, closing a gap created by a modern world in which everything appears out of stores in a somewhat abstract way, made out of unimaginable materials which seem worthless and easily disposable. Today's children see so much waste! Through the handwork classes they gain a realistic knowledge of, and a reverence for, the world of nature, and become aware of ecological problems that arise in our modern world. We need to encourage new perspectives and foster a real social conciousness.

2

The Handwork Teacher

by
Patricia Livingston

The sense of beauty implies a capacity to live in imaginitive pictures. This is something the teacher first has to learn for himself.

– Rudolf Steiner

Handwork teachers need the same foundation studies in Anthroposophy as all other Waldorf teachers. They should have a sound knowledge of child development and curriculum. They also need experience in painting, form drawing, and eurythmy to enliven their sense of color and strengthen their feeling for form and space.

Handwork teachers must be well centered, have a real interest in children, and a good sense of humor. This requires reading and working with Steiner's indications for the spiritual ground upon which the teacher establishes herself. The steps in self-development undertaken by the teacher make all the difference in how prepared she feels and how the children will respond when she stands before them in the classroom.

Continued self-education is essential, and handwork teachers should take full advantage of all educational lectures and workshops for Waldorf teachers, so that they will inwardly carry the whole life of their school. This will open doors to other areas of activity where they can take part and be helpful. Handwork teachers are often very practical, and their schedules allow time for them to carry many of the extra tasks which are so numerous in an active school. They can be excellent substitutes, help with costumes for dramatic presentations, and can be extra hands for assemblies and festivals. The planning of fairs and exhibits can also benefit from the insights of the handwork teacher and gives her valuable experiences as well as an opportunity to get to know parents. With such a background of varied contributions, handwork teachers can become very valuable, respected members of the school community.

What are the ongoing responsibilities of the handwork teacher? There are many, and she needs to be organized. If she has a busy schedule, rhythm and repetition help her to breath more easily, to be less tired, and to accomplish more. There must be time each day to go through the children's work and prepare for the next day's classes; weekly faculty meetings and after-school sessions with children also take time, and even her responsibilities at home need to be worked into the daily schedule. When I was teaching in New York, I had to do all my grocery shopping before I went to school in the morning. I had to know what the dinner was going to be and sometimes even cook the dinner before I left home.

A well-planned day or week will become rhythmical, if a teacher makes definite times for things to be done. In that rhythm I would also include time for thoughts and meditations. When we teach our classes in a rhythmical, breathing way, the children develop inner concentration and so do we.

Discipline

What about discipline? Discipline is not just a set of rules, though it does require a teacher to be consistent. It is a creative process that starts with interest in the child, leading to a deeper knowledge of what problems or characteristics lie behind his or her behavior. It is important for handwork teachers to learn to handle their own discipline problems, if they want to keep the respect of the children. Of course, they must work with the class teacher to gain insight into each child and the class as a whole. It is extremely helpful to visit main lessons and other classes to see how the children behave in different situations. One is often surprised to find that a difficult child in handwork is a star pupil in main lesson, or the other way around. Thinking ahead is important in preventing thoughtless reacting to unexpected behavior. Knowing the child is the key.

Faculty child studies and discussions with other teachers combined with one's own experiences build up one's knowledge of the child. Rudolf Steiner also suggested that teachers try to picture each child in an objective way, without judgment, before going to sleep at night. This exercise can help develop valuable constructive insights and make one more observant and able to work with the children's problems.

We are working with the child's changing consciousness. For first graders the teacher is like the sun shining over them, steady and dependable. They look up for guidance. We can still base our teaching upon the children's natural inclination to imitate. All this slowly changes as they go through the grades, and we must transform our discipline and ourselves in order to teach age-appropriately. If we work by speaking to the imaginative dream life of young children, they take in all we want to teach them in a wonderful way. However, we must be careful that in every grade, as the children begin to change, we also change and do not try to hold them at a stage to which they no longer belong. One should be well versed in the life of the children and the news of the day, so that as the children grow older, one can participate in classroom discussions in a wise and helpful way. Then, inwardly the children begin to ask, "Who is this person? How does she stand in the world?" All in all we must learn to be flexible enough to change within each day from addressing one age to another and still maintain the right kind of authority.

Working with the Temperaments

Deepening one's knowledge of the temperaments and learning how to work *with* them, and not *against* them, increases one's insights and understanding of the children. There is written material by Rudolf Steiner and others available as a background, but it is through observation and experience that one begins to gain a sense of how to work with the children and bring balance to their temperaments.

You must be extremely careful not to label a child with one temperament too strongly, or you may overlook the other three, but we can talk about extremes. I once taught a very choleric boy who was intelligent and marvelous in many ways, but he was quick-tempered and tremendously difficult in every class. He was very good at handwork and was quiet and harmonious when he was working, but if he had to wait for instructions or needed help, he could be a terror! When I looked over the handwork between lessons to see exactly what each child needed, I paid extra attention to the work of cholerics. When this boy was about to end something, I sometimes said to him at the beginning of the lesson, "When you finish what you are doing, you may have to wait five or ten minutes before I will be able to help you. You may take out your book and read if you want." Cholerics want to get ahead and be first, and they hate to wait and need to be forewarned about what will happen. For this plan to work, the teacher must always fulfill her promises exactly (he timed me with his watch). If she does, a trust is built up which will help when she deals with other problems in the future. Cholerics need to know that you are strong and definite, that you love them, and that you are not afraid of them. Then things can go well.

Melancholics often lack confidence and have a hard time deciding what to do next or what colors to use. They present a different challenge. There was a child who could never get started, because she was so overly thoughtful and concerned about what color to use. She always asked, "What do you think?" So, once I said, "Well, the blue would be nice, or you might try green, or perhaps purple. Is there another color you like?" I was less concerned about the color than giving her the confidence to make a choice. When she found she had an ally in me, she finally summoned up her courage and with great sensitivity chose the right color.

Sanguines are another problem. They pop all over the place. You often have to sit them right next to you to keep them focused and look over every other minute and say, "Do a few more stitches." They usually like sitting next to you and want to make progress but simply can't concentrate. You have to keep them interested. "Do one row, and I will do the next" sometimes keeps them going. To help a restless sanguine I would often send them on errands. In the New York City school a young first grader could take a written message five flights down to the front desk, wait for an answer, and come back up filled with satisfaction and a sense of adventure and ready to set to work. The receptionist knew how to play this game.

I gave a lot of attention to phlegmatics, because they often do not show their true being and can easily be misunderstood. It takes time and effort to get to know them and learn how sensitive and intelligent they usually are. Because their bodies seem to be asleep doesn't necessarily mean they are asleep in their heads. They can be very good knitters; they can understand and easily do heel decreases and other complicated tasks, but they are slow and often just don't like to work. They need the teacher's attention and interest. They need to hear her positive expectations to pull them out of their phlegma. Then they can shine. I often took them after school to work with them and help them move ahead. I tried to give all children alternatives to coming after school, but often they wanted to come. With most children the suggestion alone made them work much better in class, and it was not necessary to require extra time.

The Importance of Color and Design

Today, a true relationship between color, design, and function is in danger of becoming lost. The connection has become less and less visible in clothing and in the ordinary objects we use in daily life. A breadboard is shaped like a cat, the handle of a child's toothbrush takes the form of Mickey Mouse, all kinds of things are placed anywhere on clothing, and the use of color appears to have lost all sensitivity. Chaos reigns and apparently is the objective!

To encourage the development of artists for the future who will reunite color, form, and function, we must foster an impulse that will strongly connect children to the things around them in a deeper, more creative way.

Handwork and crafts offer a real opportunity to combine color and form in a vibrant way. In an Oxford lecture Rudolf Steiner said:

It is immensely important that the children come to a right experience of color. They must not paint from a palette, but from a jar with liquid color in it, color dissolved in water. Then the child will come to feel how one color goes with another, he will feel the inner harmony of colors, he will experience them inwardly.

We must bring this experience into our use of color in handwork and crafts and inspire the children to combine colors in a way that will enhance the design and form of the object being made. We see how the experience in the painting lessons is carried over into the handwork lessons, strengthening and broadening the children's involvement in color. Form drawing in its disciplined artistry also prepares them to express their own creative ideas in design.

Designs must have a relationship to the handwork projects. For instance, in embroidering a tablecloth one should leave empty the place where the dishes will go. A handkerchief would also have embroidery around the edges. Bags of different kinds should have lighter colors where the hand touches to open them and darker colors where they protect and carry what is inside. A recorder case would be the same, and so on.

There are simple color exercises one can do in handwork class with crayons to make the children more observant of color values. I asked them to make a circle filled with a light color and surround it with two more wide colored circles, putting the darkest on the outside. We then put them up on the blackboard to see which really went from light to dark. Is red darker than green? Is yellow always the lightest color? This helped the children become more aware when they made designs.

The children learn many traditional embroidery stitches as they go through the grades, but it is most important that they learn new ways of doing embroidery. For example, a space can be filled in with slanted stitches going in one direction, much as one might do in drawing a picture, and then slanted in another direction when the design calls for contrast. This technique leads to all kinds of design possibilities in the upper grades.

Gifted Children

Gifted children who do especially beautiful handwork and are able to finish comparatively quickly should be asked to do special projects. I wanted to instill the impulse of giving by suggesting they make something for the school to sell at the fair or contribute something to the school's permanent exhibits. It could also be something needed for the handwork baskets, such as a needle case or a pin cushion. Sometimes a child has a slightly negative reaction to this at first, but when others say they also would like to do it, the mood quickly changes, and contributing becomes an honor.

Older students with special abilities who have finished the class project should do a second project as well, something more advanced and suited to their individual gifts and capacities. At the same time, they should become good assistants and take time to help their classmates when needed. Interest in each other's work creates a real feeling of togetherness in a class.

The Handwork Room

What the children see around them, even when it is unconsciously taken in, has a strong influence. If they see beautiful objects and pictures, they take them into their sleep, and it works against the ugly TV images they might also bring. If the school is fortunate enough to have a handwork room, the colors of the walls and curtains should be very carefully chosen. You should put up pictures that show beautiful forms and suggest designs as found in old architecture or the Goetheanum or anything that illustrates a metamorphosis of form. You might also have a classical picture of a child or adult doing handwork and real examples of handwork up on the wall.

The way the room looks is important for the children and ultimately depends on the artistic experience of the teacher. To start with, you can always seek advice from the art and woodwork teachers, who can help you find what you need, but it is the arrangement of baskets, yarn, and colorful handwork materials that will give the room a distinctive, inviting appeal.

The Handwork Assistant

A foremost task is the work you do with an assistant. One good assistant is worth more than two or three casual helpers. You can teach large classes with one assistant if she is well trained. It is the handwork teacher's responsibility to make this possible and to help her learn what she needs to know. Time must be arranged for going through the work together each day, checking and correcting what the children have done and studying their mistakes to see what went wrong. As you discuss the children and their work, your assistant can learn the pedagogical meaning of what you are doing as well as many practical skills. Of course, she must understand the importance of confidentiality in all discussions of the children.

Every teacher should make each project before it is taught, and the assistant is no exception. In this way she learns what difficulties may arise and will be prepared to instruct and correct work quickly in class. In teaching the class, the assistant can be asked to be responsible for a small group of struggling children, while you teach the rest and hold the class together. Later, when she seems ready, you can reverse the situation and take the special children yourself while she runs the class. This can be a sobering experience for an aspiring teacher, but it is important that she learn how you have to stretch your consciousness and awareness to oversee the whole class.

In a small school one is often grateful just to have irregular volunteers as helpers who come and go and have little time. However, they, too, need guidance and can be helpful in the same way if they are interested and able to make time. I often had assistants who later went on to language teaching, class teaching, kindergarten, or handwork teaching. Any new teacher who has an opportunity to learn how to teach before taking on full responsibility is fortunate indeed. To assist a handwork or kindergarten teacher is an invaluable experience. For three years I assisted Arvia Ege, a great teacher of art and handwork and a founder of the first Rudolf Steiner School in the United States. Through her I gained experience, inspiration, and a great love of teaching. Looking back on all I learned about art, crafts, and children, and all I gained through working with other teachers, I see handwork teaching as a true path of self-development. It is also a strengthener of the will. Having had the opportunity to work with colleagues who shared the same ideals and supported my strivings was a gift for which I am eternally grateful.

The Kindergarten

I am often asked questions about handwork in the kindergartens. It is so important to understand which activities are suitable for preschool children. In the following article Dora Dolder beautifully describes the perfect way for kindergarten children to work creatively with their hands. This wonderful background is a true preparation for the handwork which follows in the grades.

3

Handwork in the Kindergarten

by
Dora Dolder

Introducing unspoiled children of preschool age to their first primitive handwork is not difficult when one appeals to their imitative capacities and their love of movement, for the will to express themselves in practical activities is a fundamental element of their lives. These initial works with their hands are different from the handwork lessons of the grade school in a basic way. In the grade school there is a step-by-step building up of practice, learning, and work. In the kindergarten there is a wondrous experimentation, imitation, and new creativity—everything is still creative play. Activity and fantasy flare forth simultaneously.

The handwork in our kindergartens begins outdoors with the actual experience of nature. A garden offers an abundance of possibilities for activity. Nature appears in the life and play of the children throughout the whole year. The children are always there, wanting to form something with their hands—out of blossoms and leaves, with pine needles and grasses, with bits of wool, fruit peels, and seeds, with sand, stones, and earth. Yes, even in winter they can model wonderfully with the snow. Just a few of these activities are briefly mentioned here. Through all their senses, the children grasp these seasonal activities from the world around them.

In spring, when the trees begin to bloom and the fir in the middle of the garden throws down its cones, there arises a game which speaks to all of the children, the wildest and also the most placid. We call it "decorating little trees." We search for a handful of fallen blossoms, flowers, grasses, and pebbles. It is easy to place these ornaments in the somewhat opened fir cones, and even the little hands which are impatient and unskilled can do it, and there soon blooms a little tree. Around these blooming trees there arise worlds. With further natural materials out of the garden pretty little things are tied together, wrapped round, placed within, braided, and built. Thanks to the power of the children's fantasies, everything comes to life, going far beyond what is physically apparent to them in the garden through their senses.

An "art" which is especially appealing to the girls, is the fastening together of leaves. For this the leaves may not be too delicate or the needles of thin twigs too coarse. This work requires care and a fine sense of the finger tips. The joy is then great when the crown, the little hat, or the little basket holds together! And if it tears, one must just quickly gather anew and begin again. This belongs to the experiences of the 5 and 6 year old. One can recognize something of their temperament through this. Overall, one must stand by helpfully. One must be attentive and yet enter in as little as possible in order not to interrupt the stream of activity, thus helping along all the broom-makers, switch-makers, grass-braiders, chive-bundlers, wreath-braiders, and so forth.

In the fall, the colorful environment inspires further lovely things to do. Here are just two examples of occupations of this season which awaken enthusiastic activity. When "grinding flour," the dry, crackling leaves are rubbed in the little fists and are added to water, bringing forth color, as if through magic. Are there children who will, with great enthusiasm, try to find out which colors can be produced by mixing water with leaves, blossoms, nutshells, or wild cherries? They will mix them in the water, stir it well, and strain it out. They may laugh and dance with joy, if they are allowed to dip snow white cloths of cotton into these colored waters. Even if their colors are pale, only a shade of brown, a tender green or a hint of yellow or red, this can be just the right thing, for later they can make little dolls of the cloths, and their faces will come alive.

These diverse, loving occupations with objects from nature stimulate the preschool child's imagination and delight in creating. The child perceives in a still dreamy empathy a multitude of forms, colors, and movements which are full of life. One should not overlook the nourishment which comes through the flow of reverence (and which is such a contrast to the stereotyped and unyielding play with Legos.) These first experiences of basic human occupations, such as searching, picking, wrapping, tying, knotting, sewing, dying, and also sowing, harvesting, grinding, and baking, come about through the child's own doing of them. He grows into life through these first combinations of play and work. These occupations grow into real abilities in grade school, where the children master the techniques of knitting mittens or crocheting. Then, a real knowledge can shine forth.

A pure and beautiful material which brings us to ever new uses is the plant-dyed sheep's wool. One can play and model with it in a beautiful way—that is quite different from working with sand, clay, or beeswax. A basket with colorful wool calls for every child's little hand to reach into it and to stay for a while, playing with these fine, gauzy, transparent tufts.

An especially beloved beginning is the making of airy balls; each child may take one tuft. These can grow when little fingers carefully pluck the wool until it becomes a big, round transparent cloud, swaying from one hand to the next. After this "snowy evening or thunder cloud play" is thoroughly enjoyed, we take the cloud between both hands and begin to round it, to turn it, to form it all around. Everybody will feel the warmth in the palms as slowly the cloud becomes smaller, and it can be made firmer until it becomes a little ball. In the hands it can be rolled and turned, going from one child to another, giving and taking, going back and forth.

Charming, never-tiring games accompanied by songs and verses will capture the youngest children, whereas the more skilled ones will invent more dramatic games. For instance, from the flat hand the little ball is blown off and immediately caught by another child! If one puts the featherlight round thing in the cup of the hand, with fingers well bent and blows—then brrh!—it cannot get away any more. It rolls and rolls, turns itself as long as the wind blows, rests for a moment, and soon tries to run again. With joyful practice each one finds out that the little ball, breath, and hand obey each other! It is easy to transform these little "turnovers." With the awakened formative force on the inside of the hand, the round thing can be formed into an egg shape. Through the slightest changes, the gesture changes. Small children are especially gifted at this.

If one now picks at the "small head" and twists the wool between the thumb and forefinger into a beak, a little bird will perch on the hand as in a nest. Although it is unfinished, or perhaps because of that, every child will be delighted and begin to converse with it. From fabric or tissue paper we can cut wings and sew them on the back with a few stitches. Finally, the whole thing can be strung on a piece of yarn and tied to a twig so that it can be guided like a marionette from above. The child will run and jump with the bird. A rich play will develop from this simple wool, made from the abilities of the hands. Many more things can be created out of this little ball by modeling it further, sewing a few stitches to fix the form, wrapping it with spun wool or sewing on some fabric.

It is always interesting to see how well-rounded lambs will roll from one child's hand, while long, prowling foxes will come from another, and plump rabbits or lean dwarves from another. In the moment of the creation they will come alive, and with the joy of playing they will be placed in further scene—the lambs belong with a shepherd, a dog and the pasture; the foxes will need their caves, the rabbits their hollow, and the dwarves their realm with Snow White.

Children who are getting ready for first grade will develop a beginning story and will weave further with objects at hand; colored cloths, rocks, roots, or stumps will be brought together, and a little stage will be built on a table or in a corner. These little figures, which are able to come forth in the spur of the moment, become part of an everyday scene or fantasy-filled picture and bring about the very best of play. Frequently, the younger ones are the grateful spectators. Open-mouthed, they live into what is in front of them, moving, speaking, and revealing.

It can happen that the performers (the 6 and 7 year olds) are not satisfied anymore with using sheep wool tufts for shepherds or kings. Special figures in their proper clothes are devised. This calls for making small dolls. Some new hand skills are to be experienced, as well as helping each other. A wool ball as round as the full moon is placed on a rectangular cloth, certainly a self-dyed one. Skillfully, it should be put over the round head held in the small fist while a neighbor ties it together with thread. From the cloth that hangs down arms and legs can be knotted.

Children who have been busy all summer long with silky, velvety, rough leaves and flowers will now touch and examine the fabrics and make their choices; a shepherd needs a cloak different from a king's and different not only in color. One cuts an approximate rectangle for these "doll clothes," and makes little folds around the neck; again a neighbor helps with tying a ribbon around it. A bunch of silk threads or sheep's wool is attached for hair with a few stitches and a knot, then eyes and mouth are drawn on—and there stands a little doll! These simplest little dolls, which only suggest the human shape, are usually loved wholeheartedly, because such a doll can do more things than the most beautiful and expensive dolls one can buy. It laughs, it cries, sleeps, leaps about, becomes ill, practically dies and then returns to school, and so forth. Why can it do all of this in flowing transitions? Because it is not perfect, only suggestive. The possibilities are open. Yes, something is created which must be continuously completed through the child's soul activities, which invent this or that and have to do it, because no stiff, finished, forceful appearance of the doll immediately puts a lock on the activity of the child. These dolls have to get yet more outfits with crown and sword, shepherd's purse, hat and crock, apron, broom, umbrella, and even a bed and house, etc. During all of this activity one should never get into creating the naturalistic or slip into criticism.

It is important that one uses beautiful, pure material to awaken the artistic senses and sensibilities. Moreover, it is important that an active adult inspire the creative forces of the children. Yet, in the kindergarten, one should not work out of adult perfectionism. To do so will hinder a child who, out of sympathy and vigor, will imitate and be clumsy. Only out of his own experience will the child acquire the right way of doing things. How ingenious and meaningful these experiences often are!

Arising from life and from stories, many toys are made over the year, gifts of primitive workmanship which show the hand of their creators. Even without being very skillful, each child of this age is gifted to do everything in gestures and movements.

The task of the kindergarten today is to prevent the drying out of this seed-like lightness and smoothness in the limbs through too early an experience in useful, "unpoetic" handwork. The educational principles of example and imitation serve as key and path to an appropriate kindergarten education. The secret of leading a kindergarten class lies in letting the children imitate as many life circumstances as possible. Just as through imitation they learn how to walk, talk, and think, so in the kindergarten age the form of the life around them should inspire and shape the child's development. Everything that is artificial, devised, or systematically divided into learning steps can only produce something wretched which will later become a weakness in the life forces.

Reprinted with permission from the Early Childhood Association of North America. This article appeared in ***Plan und Praxis des Waldorfkindergarten*s** by the International Kindergarten Association. It originally appeared in ***Die Menschenschule*** in May, 1971.

4

First-Grade Handwork

by
Patricia Livingston

Thinking is cosmic knitting.
– Rudolf Steiner

The beginning of handwork in the first grade sets the stage for all the handwork lessons to come. How you run the class in the first two years will reflect back in the upper grades. How quiet or how noisy do you expect the class to be? How do you achieve what you want? The teacher needs to have answers to these and other such questions before she begins. Handwork should be a social time, with talking, as long as work is progressing, but not loud, and periods of silence when that doesn't work. Children should be helped to develop good habits, such as handling materials with clean hands and learning not to waste anything. In the first grade we saved short ends of yarn for fringes and stuffing and looked hard and long for needles that seemed lost. We learned how to use and carry scissors to and from the box and return threads to their proper place, and so on. There is enough time to work on these habits when the children are young, and it will save time in the future. This is as much a will training for the teacher as it is for the children!

Handwork draws the will forces into the heart realm of feeling and beauty, stirring the imagination into active creation, using the will in a new way. The dawn of thinking begins to break through with the change of teeth, and the hands are ready to take on more subtle tasks as the fingers become more nimble and awake. The heart of the child is eager to make things to keep or to give away.

There should be a special mood in the classroom. It should be filled with joy and anticipation as well as reverence and patience—patience to watch things grow, to share and work together, to wait for help. The class is a small community. We need to notice and help others and care about their work as well as our own.

What is happening in the child at this age? It is a small first step in separating from his/her surroundings and beginning to look around in a different way. This is easily observed in the first-grade child where one sees the will and the feeling gradually begin to work with the thinking. Knitting is the perfect way to bring this about.

Rudolf Steiner said "Thinking is cosmic knitting," a wonderful thought upon which to meditate. One can imagine the continuous thread of thinking weaving into whole patterns of thought, and one is reminded of the many stories in fairy tales and mythology of continuous threads, such as "The Three Norns" or "Ariadne and Theseus." With these and other thoughts in mind we must try to create a nourishing environment in which the unfolding of thinking in the children can take place in the right way.

How can one bring things that will interest and inspire the children? One needs to cultivate one's own imagination in order to stimulate the imaginations of the children. It is the imaginative forces working into the thinking that make it possible for new thoughts and ideas to come into the world. Little children are very approachable when you use stories and pictorial images in teaching. Anticipation and surprise keep them involved.

Before entering a class, the teacher must have a clear picture of what she wishes to achieve, know exactly how she will proceed, and at the same time be open to what comes from the children. Well-thought out plans prepare one to deal with the unexpected and be able to quickly change direction when necessary.

There was no handwork room where I taught, so the teacher carried everything in baskets and boxes to the classroom. I entered the new first grade carrying a little golden box (covered with gold paper). I put it down carefully on the teacher's desk saying nothing about it. Then I greeted the children, had them stand up quietly, and started doing finger exercises and verses. Usually someone interrupted to say "What's in the box?" My response was "We'll find out later. Sometimes a little gnome puts things in the box. We'll see, but first we are going to warm up our fingers." In this materialistic age a child would often say "There's no such thing as a gnome." Another child almost always responded with something like, "Oh, yes, there is! I saw one in the park at the big rock!" I said little as the children listened to one another and discussed the possibilities. They each seemed to find their own relationship to the image I presented, and we continued with our work. Years later, a sixth or seventh grader passing me in the hall might ask "How is the gnome?" and "Why doesn't he bring any surprises to our class?"

When we finished our exercises, I had the children sit down again quietly. We did a lot of standing up and sitting down in the first few lessons for practice, but also to help the restless and wake up the phlegmatics!

Meanwhile, the golden box just sat in the room creating a mood of quiet anticipation. I waited until everyone was ready and then slowly took off the lid. In the box were beautiful golden threads! I carefully took them out and held them up to show the class, handling them as though they were pure gold. We were all thrilled and delighted! Then I said "If you would like to have a golden thread on your desk, fold your hands, and don't touch it until we are all ready to begin." When each child had a golden thread (golden yarn), they stood up again and learned to tie loops and bows and take them out without making knots, and also learned to take out knots when they did. We wanted the threads to look perfect before we put them away and returned them to the gnome.

I continued to use the little box for surprises. Next lesson there were golden balls, and we learned to make a magic loop (a slip knot). (It was magic, because it didn't make a knot when you pulled both ends.) Then we learned to make chains with perfect loops—not too big and not too small. They can find this difficult at first. Some make the loops so tight they can hardly pull out the chains. These are often tense or anxious children who need to relax and work more freely. The opposite are the children who work too loosely and need pulling together in many ways. This is a balancing experience. Finally, they made beautiful long chains to wear home as kings and queens.

After that, another color appeared in the box, and then one day, the little box disappeared, and I entered the class with a big golden box! It contained not only balls of yarn but wooden needles! We learned to make chains using one needle. Finally, they made twelve perfect loops which they put on the needle and were now ready to learn how to knit.

The question of making or not making wooden knitting needles with the children before starting to knit sometimes comes up. My approach was to work first through the imaginative forces, and I did not find the process of needle making particularly creative. I wanted the actual knitting to begin as soon as possible.

In the next lesson we formed a circle in the classroom with our chairs. Again, the process of doing so must be carefully worked out and repeated the same way each time.

After we passed out the work, we checked to see that our circle was really round and all was quiet again, and we were ready to begin. We took each child in turn on our laps, showed each one how to knit, holding the needles with him or her, and used a little verse from a story I had told them. (See story at the end of this chapter.) The verse went like this: "In, over, out, and off we sail, to weave a magic, golden veil." They said the verse with me as we did each stitch, and it helped them remember what to do when they worked on their own. Sometimes a child would object to sitting on our laps until he saw others doing it. Some children would happily sit on our laps all morning and needed to be pushed out at the right time. Others, too sanguine to sit still, soon said they knew how to knit, so I let them return to their seat. It took several lessons to get them all started.

In the beginning most first-grade children work with their knitting needles in unconscious bliss. As they create a large tangle, they actively and happily believe they are knitting. Slowly, they begin to notice that all is not right. Stitches are disappearing! Holes are becoming larger! They are not discouraged, because they believe their teacher can fix anything! After a few lessons they might begin to count their stitches and notice if one is missing. As if by magic, they learn to knit, at first by being shown and imitating others, but mainly through their will and feeling, and through positive expectation.

The rhythmical pulse of repetition becomes enlivened by the enthusiasm for the project being made. I didn't show samples or tell them what it would be at first. I left room for the children to use their imaginations, and so they talked about possibilities and told each other what they were making. Later I would suggest we make a scarf of many colors. This was always joyously received.

I chose the scarf because it is a simple project that first graders can work on independently, and changing colors is a great incentive to work and use the will. It is also a wonderful way to observe and learn about colors. I used clear pastels of various shades for their first project, so they would notice subtle differences, and I left out the strong dark blues, reds, and greens, which tend to draw them away from experiencing the lighter tones. It was interesting how they distinguished between different shades in color families, calling various pinks rose, orange, or red. Plant-dyed yarns are especially good to use if the colors are clear rainbow shades. Other colors become useful later.

One must always be sure the yarn is the right weight for the needles being used. It should be heavy enough for the scarf to grow quickly and at the same time be soft and pliable.

It is good to begin knitting by making something to wear, but if you live in a hot climate, there are other many-colored projects one can make with wool that will allow the children to work on their own. A ball can be made the same way as a scarf, only gathered together on each side and stuffed. A small hat can also be done by gathering at one side for a pompom, with a brim turned up on the other.

All handwork requires techniques of hiding ends of threads and yarns, so first graders learn how to tuck in ends of wool and finish everything off neatly. It is best to hide the ends as the scarf grows. It can be very tedious if you leave them all until the end of the knitting. After this they also learn to make fringes.

Once the children learn how to knit they begin noticing sweaters and other knit clothing. They often asked if I had made the sweater I was wearing, and I was glad I could sometimes say yes. They also showed me, with great pride, the sweaters their mother or grandmother had made for them.

Taking care of the handwork box is a favorite job, and it is an honor to be chosen to do it. The children learn to untangle and wind up the balls and arrange everything beautifully. They can also take turns being in charge and seeing that all the work is put away neatly when the lesson is over. By the end of first grade, many things are learned that will serve the children well in the future.

The Story

During the first few weeks before we actually started knitting, I told a continuing story at the end of each lesson. It was a special story told to me by Arvia Ege. What follows is a simple outline. It was about a princess who lived in a magnificent castle with her parents, the king and queen, and was much loved by everyone in the kingdom. She was very happy, but as she grew older she longed to go beyond the castle walls to see what was outside.

One day she found a golden key and searched until she found a little door. The key fit into the lock, and the door opened and led her outside into the woods, where she explored a new, wonderful land. Eventually she became tired and fell asleep. A woodcutter and his wife found her and took her home to their humble cottage. Here she experienced many more new things.

While she was playing in the woods one day, she noticed a golden ball. As she went to pick it up, it rolled away leaving a golden thread which she followed into a magical land. There she saw fairies dancing with golden threads weaving in and out, singing a little verse: "In, over, out, and off we sail, to weave a magic, golden veil." She watched the beautiful dance for a long time, and after a while fell asleep and later found herself waking up in the woodcutter's cottage.

The story continues, and the princess finds the golden ball, again repeating her experience. The third time that she follows the golden thread, she ends up dancing with the fairies as they weave the magic veil.

In telling the story, I made up the details as it unfolded, filling it with life and color and describing contrasts between life in the castle, the simple life in the cottage, and the heavenly experience of the magical fairyland.

5

Second-Grade Handwork

by
Patricia Livingston

All understanding begins in wonder.
– Johann Wolfgang von Goethe

Second-grade handwork also begins with a series of projects using the continuous thread. This time the children learn to crochet using bright colored balls of cotton yarn thick enough for a size seven crochet hook. Crocheting emphasizes one hand instead of two. The balance is different, although both hands are busy. It takes a new, more intense kind of concentration. This is another rhythmical, repetitive activity with the hands that strengthens the will and brings clarity to the thinking.

I always started the first lesson having the children make long chains with their fingers, a familiar task that could be easily accomplished. They worked eagerly with happy satisfaction. One should be aware and not talk to the children too much, filling them with unnecessary information. I tried to listen and live in the deeper rhythms of their world. At the end of the lesson the balls were rewound and put away.

In the next lesson they learned how to use the hook and hold the thread. The first project was almost always a pot holder, something beautiful and useful they could give to their mothers. It is not an easy project.

It requires a good deal of correcting at first to keep the sides straight. They often have to take out and re-do stitches, but they are used to that from first grade. Giving a gift is not only a wonderful gesture, but it also increases the children's enthusiasm as they think about the person for whom they are making something. The anticipation of pleasing someone cultivates altruism.

I brought only a few colors to the lesson to begin with, leaving some anticipation for new ones to come. The children learned to use a light color in the middle of their pot holder going back and forth to make a rectangular center and then learned to go around the center with increasingly darker colors.

I call second-grade crocheting "early geometry." We learn to make different forms, such as a five-cornered mat, a purse made with a circular base, a cylindrical recorder case, a ball, and so forth. It is important that these be accurately done. Although all these projects can be made by mathematical instruction, I prefer that at first they learn to sense and observe the form. I showed them how to make a corner with three stitches and asked them to look carefully at their five-cornered mat to see where the corners should go. Are the corners the same equal distance from each other? They called this a star mat and really wanted it to look right. We also looked to see if the base of a purse was round and whether a ball was spherical. This helps them experience a sense of form in a more inner way. It is amazing how well they do with these projects.

After making several required projects, they were allowed to choose other things to make, such as a spiral mat with two interweaving colors, a ball net, or something of their own invention. One boy who had made a ball was determined to make a baseball mitt. He went ahead and figured out how to do it with loops for his fingers, etc. It was amazingly constructed, and it worked! So he had a ball and mitt he could play with in the city apartment where he lived, and was very pleased.

Able children who finished their projects fast were asked to make one for the children's table to be sold at the fair. It is good for them to do things for their school. They also learned to help classmates who had difficulty in crocheting. One's gifts are there to be shared, I told them.

Crocheting provides an opportunity to work with color and form in a simple way. The children need to think about colors and get a real sense of what goes well together. They have many choices, and one must help those children who just want to get ahead and who grab the first ball they see to pause and really look and think before they choose a color. Others who are too timid to make choices can be encouraged by suggesting several colors you think would look fine. They then have the courage to choose one. Sometimes wrong choices are made, and children learn by looking back later and seeing how one color can disturb the others. This prepares them for the upper grades when they do finer work in embroidery, which requires a more subtle sensitivity toward color.

Purple was the most popular color when I started teaching, but it was hard to find. Then came the sixties, the flower children, and colorful clothing with embroidery, which made all kinds of handwork and colors available and acceptable. It was a great boost to the handwork teacher. No longer did one need to spend hours convincing parents that their boys should do handwork. The boys really loved it. Today things have changed again. Black and gray and dull colors are popular, but handwork teachers must not feel intimidated by conservative tastes and views and must retain their feeling for beautiful colors, which are so important for the children.

Later in the second grade I brought back knitting, making sure new students also learned how to knit. We made small stuffed animals, dolls and doll clothes, and many other things that I suggested they could also make at home. I offered to start them off on their home projects and help them along the way. I encouraged them to find a special basket or box and start their own collection of yarns, needles, and hooks. Many a parent told me how their children woke up early on weekends and sat in their beds crocheting. They thanked me for the extra hour of sleep it gave them!

Making things on their own when children are young develops powers of invention and creative thinking which, if continued, will increase as they mature.

Photo from Hawthorne Valley School

6

Third-Grade Handwork

by
Patricia Livingston

Children who learn while they are young to make practical things by hand in an artistic way and for the benefit of others as well as for themselves, will not be strangers to life or to other people when they are older. They will be able to form their lives and their relationships in a social and artistic way, so that their lives are thereby enriched.

– Rudolf Steiner

Third graders are less dreamy than first and second graders, but most of them still live strongly in fantasy. At the same time, they can be surprisingly down to earth. They are entering their Old Testament period and tend to see things in stark contrasts of right or wrong, good or bad, fair or unfair. What can be difficult for the teacher in third grade is dealing with many different phases of the child's awakening consciousness at the same time. Their personalities begin to stand out more, and social relationships can be less easy. The third-grade handwork curriculum helps by bringing new challenges and a variety of possibilities for them to express their individuality.

In the original Waldorf school, as in all European schools in 1919, children attended school six days a week. It was possible, therefore, to schedule two double periods a week for all elementary school handwork lessons. In our five-day week there are usually only two single periods in the lower grades and one double period in the upper classes. Compromises have been made. The little extra sewing projects suggested for first and second grades had to be left out, so in third grade I began the year with simple sewing.

It is important for young children to learn in the right way the practical aspects of sewing and making designs for their work. Making beautiful things that are useful fosters the feeling that beauty is part of everyday life and not separate from it. Beauty isn't just a picture on the wall. It should be in everything we do, in all our gestures, and certainly in everything we make.

Our first project for sewing was a small table mat. I brought beautiful solid colored squares of cotton cloth and many shades of embroidery threads to the classroom for the children to look at. It was very inspiring! Then I asked the children if they had a special place at home to put a little mat, and we talked about what they might put on it, perhaps a candle, a favorite stone, or a small vase of flowers. We discussed leaving space in the middle of the cloth for the object and creating a design to go around it.

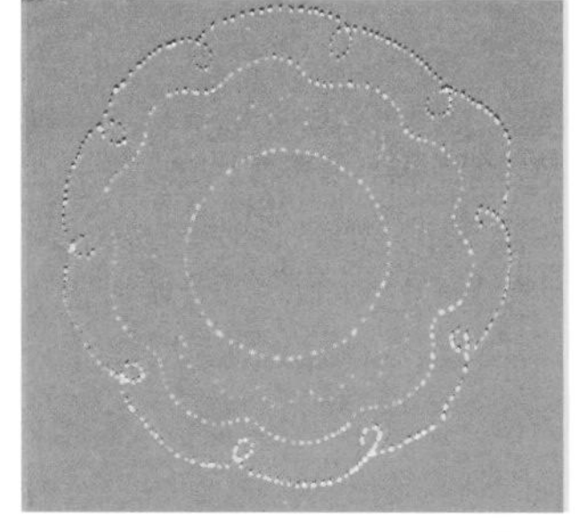

After learning how to fold a square out of a rectangular piece of paper (another important experience), they began making curved line designs with their crayons, first by copying one I made on the blackboard and then making many of their own. Colors were carefully chosen. It took several lessons to make a design good enough to transfer to the cloth. During these lessons we found time to practice threading needles (no needle threaders should be used) and making knots at the end of the thread. If you can find the right size thimble, you should teach the children to use them. That will make sewing much easier later on.

When the children start sewing their designs, they must make the stitches as even as possible. Habits are quickly formed when they start something new, so that is the time to ask for perfection. This means stitches often have to be taken out and re-done. If you do this from the beginning, they learn quickly. They also learn to end on the wrong side running the ends under the stitches instead of making a knot. We took great pride in both the front and back of our work. The mats were finished by fringing the sides of the cloth. This can be fun to do or turn to disaster if it is not carefully taught!

When everyone is busy sewing, peace reigns in the classroom. They are all working harmoniously together, yet each work is individual. These are the times when handwork teachers can give extra help to those who need it. They can also study the whole class, observe how each child goes about his work independently, and gain insights into his strengths and weaknesses.

The second project was more challenging. The children made bean bags drawing their own patterns. They were made in simple shapes which I told them should be something that flies through the air. They made butterflies, snowflakes, stars, bees, and jumping fish. Each pattern had some appropriate colored stitching on it, such as a design on the butterfly wings, or eyes and fins for the fish.

This project taught them many things. They learned to cut out the pattern, pin it to the cloth, draw a line around it, and also draw a cutting line. Next they had to cut out two pieces, sew their design, then baste the two pieces together on the wrong side, sew them together with back stitch, turn the project right side out, fill it with beans, and end it off with a colorful blanket stitch. This was a challenging project with twelve steps, or thirteen including the drawing. The children loved doing it and were happy to have something to play with when they finished. Of course, I would not outline these steps ahead of time. We just did them!

It is up to the teacher to judge whether a project is too difficult for a particular child and, if so, find a way to adjust it so he can do it, or suggest something different that he is more capable of making. The teacher must time things so that he can finish but also see that everyone is making steps forward in ability,

After the bean bags there were other projects the children could choose to make, such as a needle case, a handwork bag, or other things that would teach them new, freer ways to use color in embroidery.

With so much going on, the teacher must be able to keep calm in a sometimes chaotic atmosphere. She must be quick to see what needs to

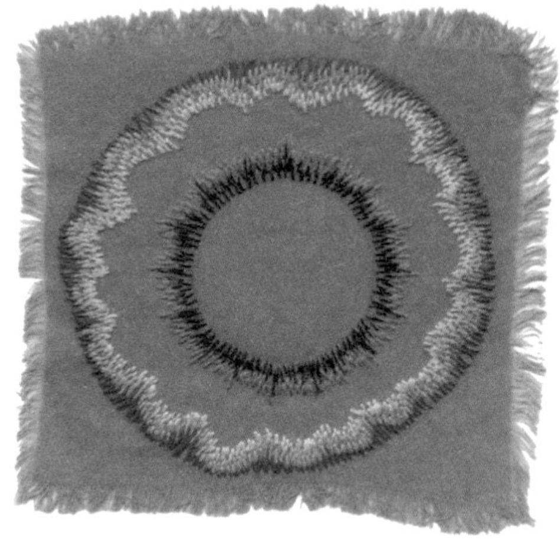

be done and fast and clear in showing the children how to do it. It is a great help if you have carefully gone through the work ahead of time.

As the teacher begins to understand and work with the handwork problems, she makes a real connection with the children, which increases her interest, love, and respect for each child. When the child feels this, it shows in his actions and ultimately in his work as well.

In discussing each grade it would be impossible to describe everything one might do, so I have given only a few examples. They are not arbitrary but are chosen to illustrate the pedagogical intent and the mood I tried to create in the classroom.

7

Fourth-Grade Handwork

by
Patricia Livingston

One should try to open the eyes of the children to all that is useful and practical, and also to the beauty of things around them. In this way they learn to "look" creatively.

– H. Hauck

When the children arrive at the age of nine, they experience a new awakening of consciousness, and they take a step forward in their thinking and in their experience of the world. They can be difficult, overly self aware, and awkward at this age. They also turn inward, and one sees their more thoughtful nature begin to appear.

In fourth grade the Norse myths are an important part of the curriculum. They mirror the soul qualities of the human being. The children enjoy the wisdom they sense coming from these tales and live in the images of light and dark, which complement their own experiences.

One of the main projects in fourth grade is cross-stitch with mirror picture designs. Doing cross-stitch is similar to making the eurythmy gesture "A" with crossed arms. It helps the children become more precise and inwardly awake and strengthens their individuality as they struggle to become themselves.

Handwork projects in cross-stitch can vary from a pine-needle pillow or pocketbook to a belt or sachet. We started the year making mirror picture designs, taking into account the project being made. I drew a vertical line on the blackboard to indicate the fold in their paper and drew a form on one side. I then asked a child to draw the mirror image on the other side of the line. I told them this design was different from what we did in third grade. We would no longer make loops or have lines crossing each other. Next I drew half of another form around the first, showing how to create a harmonious space. Again a child did the mirror image, while everyone watched carefully and commented on what was right or wrong with the results. It is difficult to do, and several children came up to try. After this everyone copied the design, added several more around it, and filled in each space with the color used to draw it. They saw how cross-stitch works with spaces, not lines. Next lesson we did the same thing with a "double" mirror picture, and then they eagerly made some designs of their own.

Making these basic designs is part of a learning process. Symmetry is an important inner exercise in seeing two sides of oneself. Copying a design helps them get started and makes them eager to make a drawing of their own. They learn how color enhances the form. Experiencing this in a simple project first will help them to express more complicated ideas of their own when they choose different projects later on.

A cross-stitched square sachet

I prefer to have the children start with a large project that needs a lot of cross-stitch and will involve them for at least three or four months. I used a large weave aida cloth and thick embroidery thread or appropriately sized wool. It is beneficial for everyone to be doing the same thing at first, using their own unique designs. There are always many different steps to learn, and it helps them to watch each other.

There are two ways to work in cross-stitch. Both are valid. One way is to put a line down the center of the cloth and build a symmetrical design counting stitches as you go along. It is important that the stitches are done correctly and evenly and that crosses are made going from right to left. A left-handed child can do the opposite if necessary. This method works well on small projects.

The other method is to transfer their own curved line design onto the graph paper by tracing it against the light on a window. They love to do this. I showed them how to transform curved lines into boxes and half-boxes. The resulting designs in this method tend to be freer artistically and more conscious of space than are designs of lines or dots.

When we worked on the graph paper, we started by transforming one-quarter of the center design and then mirroring it four ways to finish the inner form. It is important that they complete each form before starting the next. All the designs were done the same way, always consciously working with space. Half-crosses are really three-quarter crosses with the diagonal on the outside. The missing quarter is filled in with the next color.

Most children who are intellectually awake love doing cross-stitch but often find it challenging to draw beautiful free hand mirror pictures. Others who easily create beautiful designs can find concentrating on cross-stitch very difficult. This kind of work, however, helps to wake up the weak or lazy intellect and demands creativity from those who are too intellectually fixed, bringing balance to all the children.

At the nine-year change, the children often show a little less sense of responsibility about many things. Although they still love handwork, they can't always make themselves do it. They are filled with a new sense of being and are distracted by the many new things that have come into their lives. Unfortunately, television is one of them. They would like the handwork to get done, but they sometimes have a tendency to just sit and talk! This is a challenge for the teacher. The children must be strongly guided and not lose the habit of working or the experience that a feeling of accomplishment can bring. Expectations must be firmly held by the teacher. Interest and concern about their work must be expressed and help given in a timely manner.

A cross-stitched bag

Extra sessions working alone with the teacher may be necessary. If one keeps up the momentum in the class, it will prevent this tendency toward distraction, and good habits will return again!

A cross-stitched hand bag with wooden handles.

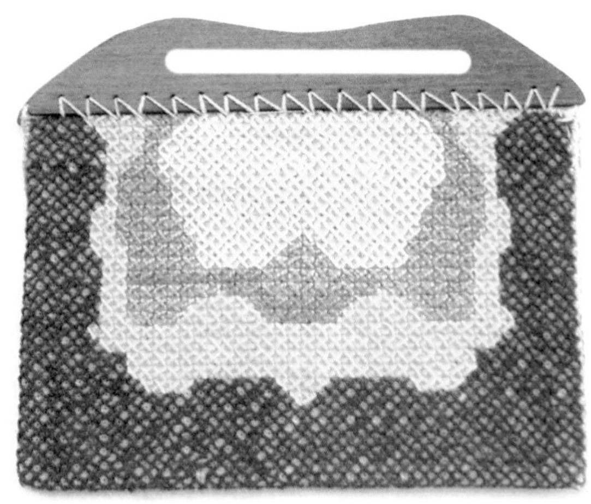

A bag with a flower motif

A pencil case

8

Fifth-Grade Handwork

by

Patricia Livingston

In a Waldorf school the boys and girls work together quite contentedly. Even if you look at the finer details, you will not find it easy to guess whether an object has been made by a boy or a girl.

– Rudolf Steiner

Fifth grade is a wonderful year in handwork. The children go back to knitting at a time when they are entering a more balanced stage of development. Most of them love to knit, and they enjoy the new challenge of working with four needles. They like reminiscing about first grade and joke and tease about the gnome. New children who can't knit need special attention from the teacher, but there are always many classmates who want to initiate them into the magical art of knitting!

Fifth graders should make something to wear that takes the shape of some part of the body. The feet are a good starting place for this age, when they begin to stand more firmly on the ground. Socks, with the intricate shaping of the heel, involving mathematical progressions, are the perfect project for them. Making socks calls on their intellect and on an active will, and also

allows for periods of harmonious, social knitting. It is a good experience for them to make something ordinary that they use every day. They become curious about their store-bought socks, especially the heel, and want to see how well or how poorly they are made. Even new knitters can make socks, if they have extra help to get them started. They really prefer to do what their classmates are doing.

We used beautiful skeins of colored worsted yarn for the socks, and also small balls of color for putting stripes in the cuffs. Choosing a color always makes the children eager to get started. The socks were used for skiing or skating or just for cold winter days. I encouraged them to use colors they really liked and would wear. Some choices were very unconventional! Temperaments were often expressed in their selections.

The weight of the yarn and the size of the needles are extremely important in making this project a success. If the needles are too thick or too thin, knitting can be difficult and discouraging. They lose interest, and progress is slow. Accomplishment is a necessary incentive to keep going.

Each child is given four needles and is responsible for replacing them if they get lost. In the first lesson they start by using two needles and some old yarn and learn how to cast on twelve stitches by knitting them on, and then begin their practice piece. They do two inches of knitting, two of purling, and two of ribbing (knit two, purl two). With double periods, most of them should finish this in two lessons if they don't waste time. The very slow ones, of course, will need extra time and attention, but they will do much better if they don't get too far behind. Finally, the great moment comes, and they begin their socks, learn how to knit on four needles, change colors, and tuck in ends for each cuff stripe.

The children make little books and write down each step for making socks as they go along. They need these instructions for their second socks. For some this took too much time, and I thought it more important that they spend the lesson knitting instead of writing. However, everyone was expected to copy the heel and toe decreases which I wrote on the blackboard, so they would have them when they were working at home.

Knitting in fifth grade is so social and relaxing that the children need limits and rules for classroom behavior, such as: "You may talk softly, if you are working." "If you can't do both, you must be silent," or "If you are behind in your work, sit alone for ten minutes and catch up," or the like. It helps to have a touch of humor when you speak to them, but never use sarcasm. When you teach a class for four or five years, you build up a wonderful relationship of trust and respect. They know what to expect from their teacher. One can be firm about rules and expectations, when they know you are always ready to help and encourage them. Much of the teacher's energy goes into creating this harmonious working situation. One also needs specific goals for individual children. Your interest is important in keeping them involved. All socks must be finished by the end of the year!

The handwork teacher also has certain self-requirements and goals. She must learn by heart how to turn the heel, decrease the heel, decrease the toe, weave the toe, and be able to dictate them—sometimes all at once. The children love to see her do it! Some students become so good at these things that they can be depended on to help at any time.

Photo from Great Barrington Rudolf Steiner School

In the fourth and fifth grade the children are allowed to work on their handwork at home. However, there need to be real consequences if they forget to bring it back on handwork days. In class, I had them do other work, if they forgot their socks. I sometimes asked them to start the second sock for a very slow student or copy the decreases for someone. They were expected to make up their own knitting time at home. Those who finished their socks went on to all kinds of other knitting projects, some quite advanced, such as a baby sweater for a sibling or even a patterned sweater for themselves. For this they bought their own yarn and had to convince me they would finish at home, if it was not done by the end of the year.

As the children come to the end of fifth grade, one can see they are ready to work much more independently on individual projects, which is what they will be doing in sixth grade.

9

Sixth-Grade Handwork

by
Patricia Livingston

Handwork must be judged not just aesthetically but pedagogically. It often happens that a piece of rather dull, but painstaking work, speaks more of the inner progress made by a child than does a piece of work more pleasing to the eye.

– H. Hauck

In the sixth grade the children are begining to enter pre-adolescence. They have a stronger sense of self and are finding a more independent relationship to the world around them. At the same time, they inwardly experience a new depth of feeling. Often there is much turmoil in their souls. They are losing some of the wonderful harmony of the fifth grader. Something new and interesting is needed in handwork to hold their attention.

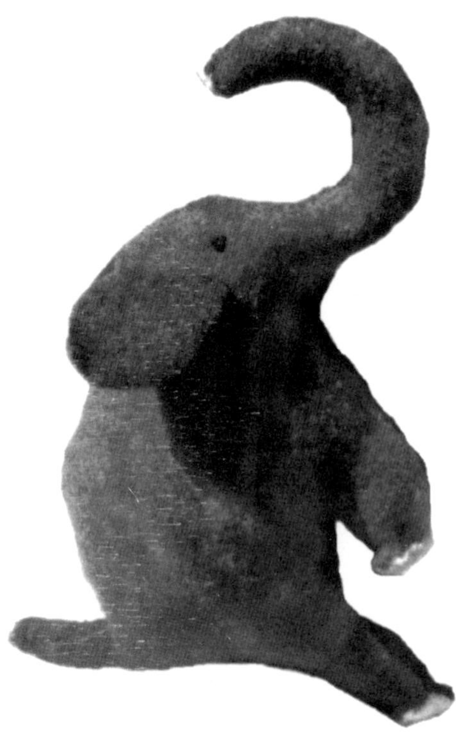

They have made small animals in knitting and crocheting, studied animals in fourth grade, and live with and love the live animals around them. What a wonderful background for the challenge of making a stuffed animal! This project requires abilities of all kinds—the artistry to draw a beautiful animal, the concentration to follow instructions carefully, and the imagination to picture how a three dimensional figure can come about in sewing.

Rudolf Steiner spoke of the difference between carving and stuffing an animal. In carving one works from the outside, taking away wood, stone, or clay and bringing forth and revealing the animal that is within. In soft handwork one ensouls the animal, stuffing and shaping it, giving it character as one molds it from within. This project comes at just the right time for the children, who are beginning to wake up in an astral sense and don't quite know what to do with their feelings. When they feel misunderstood by adults, their love and trust often flows into their animals. "My dog is the only one that understands me!" has frequently been said by a child of twelve during a moment of dramatic crisis. Making a stuffed animal is a loving gesture. The children pour their feelings into their work, and it is very satisfying. They actually play with their animals, hug them, and take them home, and then, like first graders, they want to bring them to school to put on their desks!

To begin this project, each child chooses an animal and draws a picture of it—in its natural environment, if possible, having some gesture of movement. These are done in profile. Then we discuss their choices as to their appropriateness and possibilities for a stuffed animal. In a handwork class in Stuttgart, a teacher, with the help of the students, once drew a herd of elephants on the blackboard. Then each student chose one from which to make a pattern. This can be seen in a photograph taken when the animals were finished. Inspirations such as this help to keep everyone actively and happily involved!

The teacher must be sure that each child chooses an animal that he can do successfully. Horses are often popular, but an animal with long thin legs is difficult for some children to make. They should experience working on a four legged animal, but there are other easier choices, such as bears or rabbits, that can also be made. Temperament often guides the children in their choices, but sometimes they choose what is opposite to themselves. That is always interesting! Perhaps a gentle kitten would really like to be a lion!

*Photo from **Handwork and Handicrafts** by Hedwig Hauck*

Next the children make a pattern from their picture on a piece of paper larger than their drawing and cut it out. Questions arise. How will it stand? How do we fill it out? Then they learn how to make gussets for shaping the animal and cut out and label all the needed pieces. This is an important process that can be used in making clothes later on.

Meanwhile the teacher has been collecting materials resembling animal skins and furs for years, asking her friends to save interesting old wool skirts or coats in appropriate weaves and colors, pieces of fur or leather, rough cotton, and other natural cloth continuously building up her animal collection. Perhaps one of these pieces has already been the inspiration for an animal. Now the final choice is made, and the work begins.

Every step in this project will determine how close to the original concept this animal will come. The shape will be spoiled by sloppy work. Therefore, as the work progresses, close observation and correction by both teacher and child of the details in cutting and sewing are necessary to bring this animal to birth. When all this is done and the stuffing with wool begins, the children will feel how worthwhile their efforts have been.

The animal is the main project in sixth grade, but if sufficient time has been given to handwork and crafts in the upper grades, other things can also be made. Dolls and puppets are also good for the children to make, and sewing clothing for them will be excellent practice for hand sewing in seventh grade. One can experiment with different kinds of embroidery and ornamentation, which will lead to inspired designing for clothing or costumes in the next two years.

10

Seventh-Grade Handwork

by
Patricia Livingston

It is indeed true that I am as good or as bad as my ideas of the world and myself are, for I act according to those ideas, bringing them to expression in the way I live and in what I do.

– Dr. Michaela Glöckler

In the seventh grade the children enter the artistic flourishing of the Renaissance and the rebellion of the Reformation both in the curriculum and in their own development. They discover their incredible diverse aesthetic capabilities as well as their own awakening powers of thinking and protesting. In their artwork they often become extremely creative and make elaborate designs, and they certainly are competent in working with color.

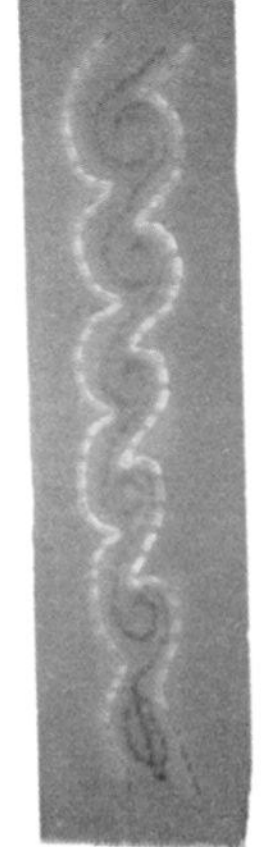

Bookmarks

This year they are ready to do projects that would not have been expected of them in the years before. This is a year when they are expected to hand sew really well and make a garment to wear. First, they create a design and then carry out that design in all its details. They learn to use embroidery in many different ways. The whole idea of transferring an artistic hand-drawn design onto a piece of cloth for something to wear is a new experience. They study how embroidery designs can enhance clothing, if one is conscious of how and where they are placed. Designs that go around the neck, the waist, and the hem should not be the same but should metamorphose and change, so that the neck design points to what is below, the hem to what is above and the waist to both directions. One often sees good examples of this in Norwegian sweaters made by those artistic knitters of the past.

The clothing the students make should be simple, and they should make their own patterns. Today's fashions make that easy to do. Original designs for shirts and tops with colorful embroidery for both boys and girls should be encouraged. Different ways of putting a personal touch on a simple garment can be an interesting challenge. Once the practical aspect is done, how can we bring an aesthetic to it which moves it a step forward toward beauty? Buttons and buttonholes colorfully embroidered or crocheted can be used as beautiful ornamentation. All the children should learn how to make them. A small interesting touch of color on a pocket or a sleeve can make as strong a statement as an elaborate embroidered design.

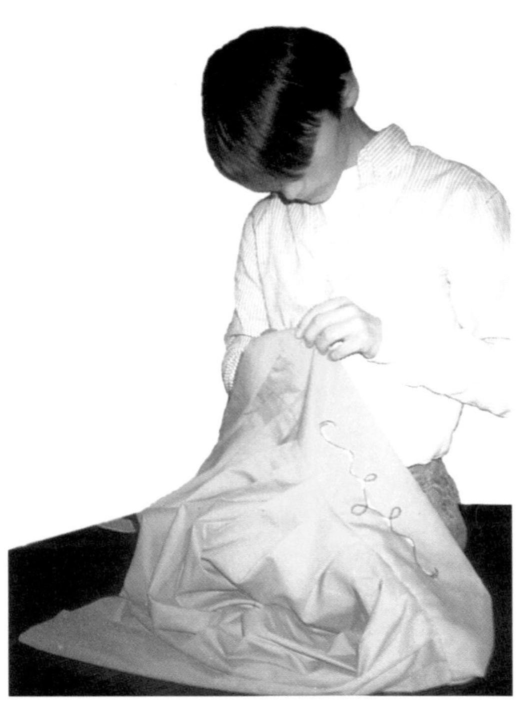

Photo from Great Barrington Rudolf Steiner School

Vests are full of possibilities for creative design. Practical aprons for carpenters or gardeners, carefully measured for tools, with some colorful stitching added somewhere, are fun to make. Cooking aprons ought to be personally designed and embroidered with the personality and tastes of the wearer in mind!

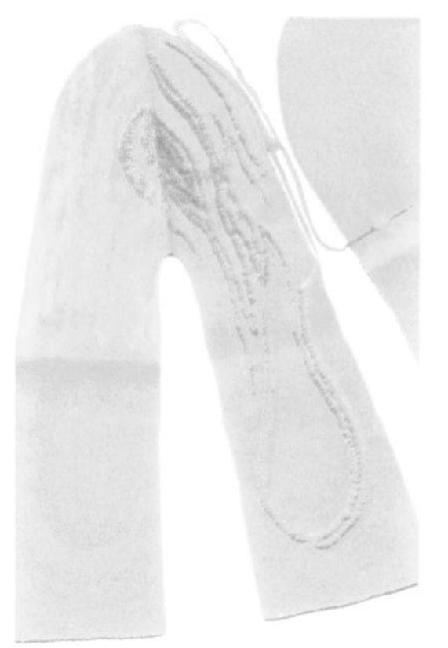

The beginning of embroidery on a pair of slippers.

Many suggestions have been made for extra projects, but with less class time than the original six-day schools, only a few of our students finish their first project in time to make them. Slippers are a wonderful project. By tracing around the foot and making a pattern to fit it, the children become aware of the bone structure and the asymetrical shape of their feet. Embroidery designs for slippers can take this into account in a beautiful way.

In the first years of the Rudolf Steiner School in New York City, the children learned to make marionettes in woodwork, dressed them in handwork, wrote a play, learned it by heart, painted the scenery, made the props, and then practiced manipulating and breathing life into the marionettes. All this ended in a wonderful performance—truly an enviable Renaissance project for a seventh grade.

Slippers have been embroidered with many unique patterns.

11

Eighth-Grade Handwork

by

Patricia Livingston

Out of their ranks can come technicians and artists who will know how to solve problems and tasks set for us.

– Rudolf Steiner

Knitting, crocheting, sewing, embroidery—what could possibly come next for eighth graders who are always looking for something new and interesting? What does come next is the possibility of using many of their previously learned crafts on a piece of clothing made with the help of an electric sewing machine. This is an exciting challenge.

The eighth-grade curriculum brings the students into the industrial revolution where machinery replaced much of the handmade work. It is now appropriate that they learn to do sewing on the sewing machine. However, it is important that the students first be introduced to an old-fashioned treadle machine, if you can possibly locate one. The visible working of this machine allows the students to see and understand what is happening. They experience how to use their arm to start the wheel turning while coordinating their legs and feet on the treadle and finding the rhythmical motion that will keep the machine going. If they learn this technique first, they will have a very real appreciation for what an electric machine can do. In some ways an electric machine is also difficult to use, but its efficiency is really a joy.

The students should also understand how an electric machine works and know what to do when something goes wrong, and simple things can easily go wrong. When the thread comes out of the needle and disappears, how do you get it back? How do you re-thread the whole machine, change the bobbin, and get it started again? The electric sewing machine goes very fast. There is no time for dreaming. The students have to practice sewing on a line and learn how to handle the cloth. They must really know the fabrics they are using. We always tried to use natural fabrics, and we started with shirts made out of cotton. It is a good first project, as cotton is easy to sew. Afterwards, the students might try making something out of silk or another material. (The children need to be guided by a parent or teacher when they go out to buy their material.) A good sewer might go further and make a jacket or a pair of trousers. I once knew an art student who was very poor and couldn't afford to buy clothing, so he figured out how to cut out a pair of pants and jacket for himself, sewed them up by hand, and wore them daily!

Photo from Great Barrington Rudolf Steiner School

In eighth grade the students also learn to use bought patterns. They must learn how to read them, how to put them together, and how to place each piece carefully on the cloth so that they all fit. Pinning, cutting, and basting are all specific detailed work that requires patience. It is not easy to make something for themselves that really fits. They need to try things on, observe, and help each other.

The students will have ample opportunity to add original embroidery to all they make and should be encouraged to do so. The teacher must inspire them and teach them how to experiment in drawing and in making samples of their own.

Have no illusions about what is asked of the teacher in order to make all this happen in a positive way. Though the students are older and often say they know what to do, they still need detailed supervision and encouragement to keep them going. The teacher must look over their work and check their progress before each class to avoid disastrous mistakes, and be ready to help them quickly and see that they work hard during the lesson. Achievement in one lesson makes them eager to return to work in the next. Keeping them focused is very important.

Other small handmade projects that the students can work on at home should also be done during the year. Intricate braiding and different ways of making belts could be learned. They can also make beautiful headbands and design and sew details on hats and costumes for their plays. It would certainly be good to teach them how to mend their clothing!

At the end of eighth grade one can talk with the students about all they have learned since first grade. They will be amazed if you try to list the many things they have been doing in handwork. We want them to experience a warm sense of satisfaction in all they have achieved. The first eight years of handwork have not only enhanced the students' capacity to be active in the world and taught them to express themselves artistically, but have also strengthened and brought clarity to their thinking.

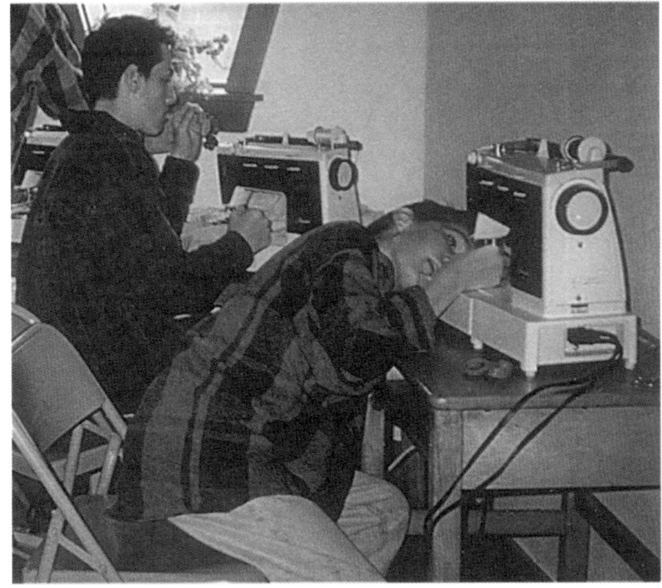

Photo from Great Barrington Rudolf Steiner School

12

Teaching Practical Arts in the Waldorf Elementary Grades

by
David Mitchell

I am not a thing, a noun. I seem to be a verb, an evolutionary process, an integral function of the universe, and so are you.
– Buckminster Fuller

The important thing is not to stop questioning.
– Albert Einstein

At the beginning of the twentieth century most people lived their lives in a close relationship to the earth—a father was usually either a farmer or a laborer. From their rural settings they performed chores, experienced their parents working, cultivated their *will* life (learned how to be effective using their hands), and came to school for the purpose of learning how to think.

Today the situation has reversed. Most students live in urban settings, and their parents leave home to go to "work." The activity of the parents' work is invisible to the child, and the direct results are not always experienced or directly appreciated by the family. Life and work have become abstractly separated.

At the same time, children are flooded with information, and their thought-life is constantly, even excessively, stimulated, putting stress on their nervous systems. It is an error to consider this information to be education! Rather it produces a type of pseudo-thinking which neither exercises nor satisfies the soul. In addition, many students lack rhythm in their lives and have no meaningful tasks to occupy them. The task of learning to "work" and to direct the *will* has been passed over to the schools.

The Waldorf handwork and practical arts curriculum strives to address this problem. Today's students need to be taught to activate their full capacities—to apply their thinking and to see the results. They are desperately in need of developing practical skills to build their self-confidence, self-reliance, and independence.

Accomplishing tasks with the hands serves to build confidence in each child. This is also a key to academic success. The children engage in a process of practical application where they "learn how to learn." Woodworking, for example, comes into the curriculum at a time when the children are developmentally ready to develop new interests and new skills. The more interests and skills we can develop in the children, the more we can help them to live on the earth and cease to be victims of a technology-based culture. The Waldorf practical arts curriculum plays an important part in the transition from play to work. The children need to experience that work is wonderful. Also, these classes are a time when the teacher can lead them to feel the joy of being altruistic, as they make projects for friends and loved ones.

Woodworking is taught from grades 4 (or 5) to 12 in a Waldorf school. The grade to begin varies, e.g., schools in rural areas observe that where the children use their hands a lot in daily tasks, they are ready to begin woodworking in the fourth grade. I taught in a school where we did this. However, my preference has always been to begin in the fifth grade.

Before looking at the development of the woodworking curriculum, let's look at some of the characteristics of the material we will work with—wood. First, we can look at the unique characteristics of different varieties of wood; we can examine the different textures, colors, softness or hardness, and density.

Understanding Wood

We have hard wood and soft wood. Some woods have a wide patterned grain, while others have a tight straight grain. Each wood will reveal to the carver its fast or slow growth, its moisture or dryness, its capacity for splintering, and each will call for different strokes with the gouge as well as different finishing techniques. For example, in carving a piece of elm students learn how to work with a wood that has a twisted, unpredictable grain. They are required to observe and teach themselves as they progress with their work.

Each wood has a personality, color, smell, and texture. For example, the hardwoods are close-grained, take a high polish, and they have broad flat leaves (ash, maple, beech, elm, oak, chestnut, linden/ basswood). The softwoods are easy to work with, have a loose grain, and have narrow, resinous leaves (pine, fir, hemlock, and redwood).

Some other qualities of woods are:

oak — rugged strength
elm — twisted grain, rugged and flexible
walnut — rich, dark, and warm, polishes beautifully
ash — bends easily, holds its bark
beech — light, speckled and playful, yet strong
cherry — color portrays inner warmth
pear — hard and brittle, good for detail
apple — strongly marked grain
lilac — powerful color changes in the wood
ebony, lignum vitae — waxes itself, heavy

Examples of different woods can be passed around so the children can make their own observations and contribute to the conversation. The important thing is to arouse their interest in wood as a material to be worked with. I explain that hickory, lignum vitae, rock maple, and beechwood make the best mallets (their tight growth resists compression as it is used to strike a chisel handle), while ash, boxwood, mahogany, sycamore, walnut, and hazel make the best handles (their grain provides for elasticity—they will flex and not easily snap).

The children should understand how trees grow from a sprout to a sapling to a full tree, and they should have an imagination of how a forest grows and replenishes itself. There are many ways in which a forest contributes to our welfare: when it is dark, the trees release oxygen for us to breathe; they provide building materials for our homes; their fruit and seeds become food for both humans and animals; the animals make homes under and in their canopy. The forest's dense, umbrella-like covering slows the run-off of rain, and the rich leaf-molded floor holds water like a sponge, allowing it to slowly seep underground to join streams and ponds.

Along with expanding the children's awareness of the natural world, the teachers in the practical arts curriculum in a Waldorf school have other areas of responsibility.

Safety

A first priority is to insure safety in the work area. Every space should be clean, free from clutter, and have adequate full-spectrum lighting (natural, if possible). At least one appropriately coded fire extinguisher must be present along with a first-aid kit, the inventory of which should be restocked on a monthly basis, or sooner, if necessary. Every practical arts teacher should have training in basic first aid. All flammable substances and supplies must be stored in suitable locked metal containers, and all rags must be properly disposed of on a daily basis. Tools and machines should be clean, adequately stored, with manuals accessible. The conscious teacher carries the safety of the work place as a priority at all times but most especially at the beginning and conclusion of every work day.

Guiding Conversations

In the younger grades one can sing with the children as they work. The singing brings about a regularity in the breathing. The rhythm in the song creates bodily harmony and allows for efficient movement. This is the reason for sailors singing sea shanties, as they hauled up the heavy anchor, or farm workers singing as they monotonously picked cotton or fruit. Rhythm helps keep the body from becoming tired.

> *Try to establish a connection between instruction in music and singing and handicrafts. . . . This connection should exist. It would greatly benefit the children. Every kind of work started out from music. Today this is not heard any more, but if you went into the country and heard the peasants threshing, you would hear the rhythm in their handling of the flail. This kind of rhythm is needed by us. Then we would get the spirit back into working.*
>
> – Rudolf Steiner

In the younger grades, I liked to tell humorous stories that continued over to the next lesson. This created a feeling of expectation when the children came to class. It also relaxed those youngsters who were tense.

However, one of the more important accomplishments can be in guiding and developing the conversations. There are certain conversations one might want to avoid, such as those involving violence on the television or from the movies. If it does come powerfully into the classroom through the experience of the children, the teacher has to recognize that the children need to process and digest the images. Thoughtful questions and discussion can settle the students, if the teacher has patience and wisdom.

A wonderful aspect of Waldorf education is that the atmosphere in the schools is constructive and happy. No matter what the children are exposed to in the rest of the world, in the school setting they receive something positive that they may carry with them through life. In the woodwork class many of their life experiences can be openly talked about and digested. The observant teacher can be a quiet counselor and guide.

I tried to establish, and maintain, a high level of conversation in my classes. This involved observations and stories about nature, questions about what they were doing in main lesson or where they had traveled on the holidays. It is an art to be able to sustain a decent conversation and involve everyone. Being able to to listen to each other is something that is learned. Both the handwork and the practical arts teacher help to develop these important social skills of conversation and listening.

If the conversations became too loud, I would just say, "Okay, we will all become quiet for seven minutes and nineteen seconds," or some such ridiculous number. I would then accurately clock the quiet time, while they enjoyed being able to focus on their projects with deepened concentration. Almost always, when the time was up, they would be more peaceful and more fully engaged in their work.

If one of the children used bad language, I would just say tactfully, "Those words aren't welcome in this class. They float up to the corners of the ceiling and make the room dirty." Every word one utters can have an effect on the entire group. Group awareness is a developed social skill that must be learned. We would learn new phrases to vent frustration like, "Oh diddles!" or "Ten thousand curses!" It was fun!

You can't make rules about how to guide conversations. Rather, you must emulate a conductor trying to direct an orchestra. You have to deal with what happens in the moment. It depends on the class, it depends on who's absent that day, and so on.

If we teach our classes in a rhythmic, breathing, emotionally relaxed atmosphere, it will be a strength to the students and will give them tools for life.

Ecology

Care and respect for materials leads to moral and social responsibility. The manual arts studio or classroom should be a model of ecological awareness and wakefulness. Every scrap of everything can be resurrected and have a purpose. Sticks can be transformed into buttons, scraps of leather can become flexible hinges, sawdust can stuff puppets or make putty when mixed with white glue, and pieces of hardwood can become inlays.

One of the unwritten rules for a handwork or woodwork teacher is that they must have some tendencies toward being a packrat. While this can drive spouses to distraction, the children inwardly delight when they see a novel use for what might ordinarily be thrown away.

I created bins, bottles, and boxes to recycle all our scraps. When I could foresee no use for something, or when my "Pippy Longstocking" tendencies of finding a "treasure" around every corner started to clutter things up too much, the scraps could always go into the wood stove to keep us warm. All of this was carefully and consciously explained to the children.

One of my delights was when the children came running to the shop to fetch some odd thing they needed for a play or a class project, because they knew there was a good chance of finding it, or making it, from our collection of recyclables.

Cultivating Altruism

> *One of the tasks of people living in North America is to develop the capacity of altruism.*
>
> – Rudolf Steiner

Working in crafts allows the anticipation of pleasing someone to whom we would like to give our project. The projects provide "real" gifts for the children for birthdays or other holidays. Because they are made with such devotion, the recipient usually treasures them.

In the upper elementary grades we can build into our curriculum a community activity which allows the students to use their considerable skills for the common good. Several of these projects are outlined in the chapters which follow.

Thinking

Thought activity is cultivated through an approach to the subject where the phenomena are studied and evaluated before conclusions and theories are drawn. This process leaves the student free to develop and exercise the capacity for judgment and discrimination.

Dynamic thinking requires movement. Wordsworth and Goethe both created their most beautiful poems while walking. In the crafts classes the children are constantly in motion. The children inwardly imitate the techniques taught by the teacher, and this flows as a formative force into their hands. An adult can notice that the power with which children observe and then create is not born out of the intellect, but is the result of an interaction between sense observation and will activity. I will address the education of the "senses" at the end of this chapter.

All active limb work requires blood movement. When the children are fully engaged, you can see that their cheeks are red, flushed with blood, and from this movement bodily warmth and lactic acid are produced.

Thinking produces the opposite—it stirs our body chemistry toward the alkaline pole. Thinking requires coolness. Too much heat (fever), and one hallucinates and doesn't think properly. The children become pale when they are engaged in thinking for extended periods of time. Thinking originates from our nerves, the only non re-creating cells in our body—our nerves are that part of our cellular life which is closest to death. We need to balance these two polarities of thinking and will activity. The practical arts, and all active working of the will, produce a constructive body chemistry.

When we are working with our hands, our thinking becomes vitalized. When children understand that there are many ways of completing a given task, and that mistakes can be corrected, then they develop more flexible thinking. As children observe their skills improving, they become flooded with self confidence.

Awakening Moral Judgment

There is an intimate connection between crafts and morality. Craftspeople, in order to be true to their material, have to be centered and focused on their intuitive processes in relation to the stone or wool or wood. Craftwork cannot be done in a hurry. Care and patience must be integrated. Craftwork is basically a differentiated, organized way of incarnating spirit into matter.

In many ways morality is the opposite of thinking. Rudolf Steiner commented that "morality is actually a problem of *will* and not of thinking." The *will* is hidden to our consciousness; it is asleep deeply within us. Our thinking is universal—our *will* is that part of us which is most truly individual. Moral codes were created for mankind by religious leaders, but morality remains an individual experience. We own our own morality. In our bodies our *will* creates instinct. It is our *will* in our physical body which creates our digestion, respiration, and heartbeat. It is our *will* in our feeling life that creates passion, desires, and cravings. That *will* which works in our higher nature, our ego, creates motivation. It is motivation which leads us to morality. As we are motivated to strive in our craftwork, we are touching upon the kernal of morality—the wish to do better, to approach perfection. Morality is being true in oneself toward something. The crafts awaken the capacity to form moral judgments. One must constantly make determinations on how to proceed with the work at hand. Mistakes must be corrected and worked with, because we don't throw things away or start over, except in dire circumstances. The spoon with the hole carved through the bottom is transformed into a salad fork, and so on. Thus, the authority should flow out of the work itself and not necessarily always from the teacher. This will allow the student to develop more respect and love for the subject and will allow the teacher to spend more time on the pedagogical tasks at hand. The attitude in the classroom or studio develops integrity in the children when the expectations are clear and well defined.

The teacher strives to guide the students in such a way that a feeling for "what is right" is established. Then this is repeated until it becomes habitual. This process is the foundation for moral development.

The practical arts transform the "play" of the child first by awakening aesthetic formation, then by developing the capacity for practical formation, and finally to experience the joy of work itself.

Educating the Senses

Living is learning. When we are most alive, using most fully our energies, senses and capacities, we are learning the most.
– John Holt

The texture of the smooth wood, the smell of a freshly sawn log, the smell of the aromatic oils from a crushed leaf of sweet fern or eucalyptus, the odor of a burning pine cone, are all part of the education of the senses. We need to provide as many nourishing sense experiences for the children as we can.

The children can be taught how to put on a blindfold and identify trees by the feel of the bark. They can smell a fresh sassafras root dug from the soil and then boil it into a tea that they can taste. They can experience the smooth surface of a piece of wood cut by a sharp knife, or plane, by stroking it against their cheeks. They can eat a winterberry or chew a pepermint leaf. They can balance themselves and walk on a fallen tree; they can dig a handful of fresh leaf mold and smell its earthy richness. A full sense-experience of their environment will give them confidence in their surroundings.

The twelve senses, as described by Rudolf Steiner, and a few practical experiences which can stimulate them in the crafts class, are listed below:

The 12 Senses

Sense of touch

(where we materially relate to the external world)	These first four senses are where a sense is entirely within the organism.	Texture of wood, smoothness, roughness. Coolness of stone and metal.

Sense of life

(where we sense our wellness or sickness)	When we go more inward, we have the sense of life.	Quiet focus on project. Working outdoors in the fresh breeze.

Sense of movement

(where we perceive the movements of our limbs each other)	When we go still more inward, we have the sense of movement.	Sawing, rasping, filing, chopping, gouging, relative to eye-hand coordination is brought into conscious rhythm.

Sense of equilibrium

(where we find our relation to above, down, left, and right)	When we go even more inward, we have the sense of equilibrium or balance.	Different body positions allow the whole upper body, not just the hands, to be involved. i.e., the rocking movement in rasping where the entire upper body synchronizes into the activity.

Sense of smell

(we merely perceive through this sense to outside world)	These next senses are where we pass outside of ourselves. The sense of smell is the most outward.	Each wood has its own individual odor. The polish is highly aromatic.

Sense of taste

(where we bring the outer world within ourselves)	A deeper penetration inward is the sense of taste.	Many leaves, roots, and bark have distinctive tastes.

Sense of the sight

(where the world enters us as a picture)

A still deeper penetration is the sense of sight

Sharpened observation notices contours, the evenness of the bevel, and the flatness of a plane's surface.

Sense of warmth

(where we have an intimate relationship with the outer world and experience the quality of an object as cold or hot)

An even deeper penetration is the sense of warmth.

Friction produces warmth in the wood. Limb activity produces warmth in the body. The stone takes on and stores the temperature of its environment and is usually experienced as cool.

Sense of hearing

(where we experience the inner texture of external things)

The next penetration inward is the sense of hearing.

All the activities of pounding, scraping, sanding, sawing, have individual identities depending upon the medium being worked with.

Sense of word

(where sounds become imbued with meaning)

The sense of word is still a deeper penetration inward.

The cultivation and conscious construction of proper conversation.

Sense of thought

(where we develop a living connection with the word)

The sense of thought is deeper, still—it shapes the word.

The conceptual process of conceiving a design or figuring out the mechanics of a moveable toy or the geometry of a dovetailed joint.

Sense of Ego

(where we gain a true perception of another person's ego)

The deepest sense is when we give up ourselves and truly perceive another human being.

Group interaction and heightened social awareness is achieved.

While the practical arts can enhance and train the senses, music and eurythmy are the arts which weave the senses into a beautiful tapestry.

Storage space for projects should be artistically considered.

An organized, brighly lit shop inspires work.

How a Tree Grows

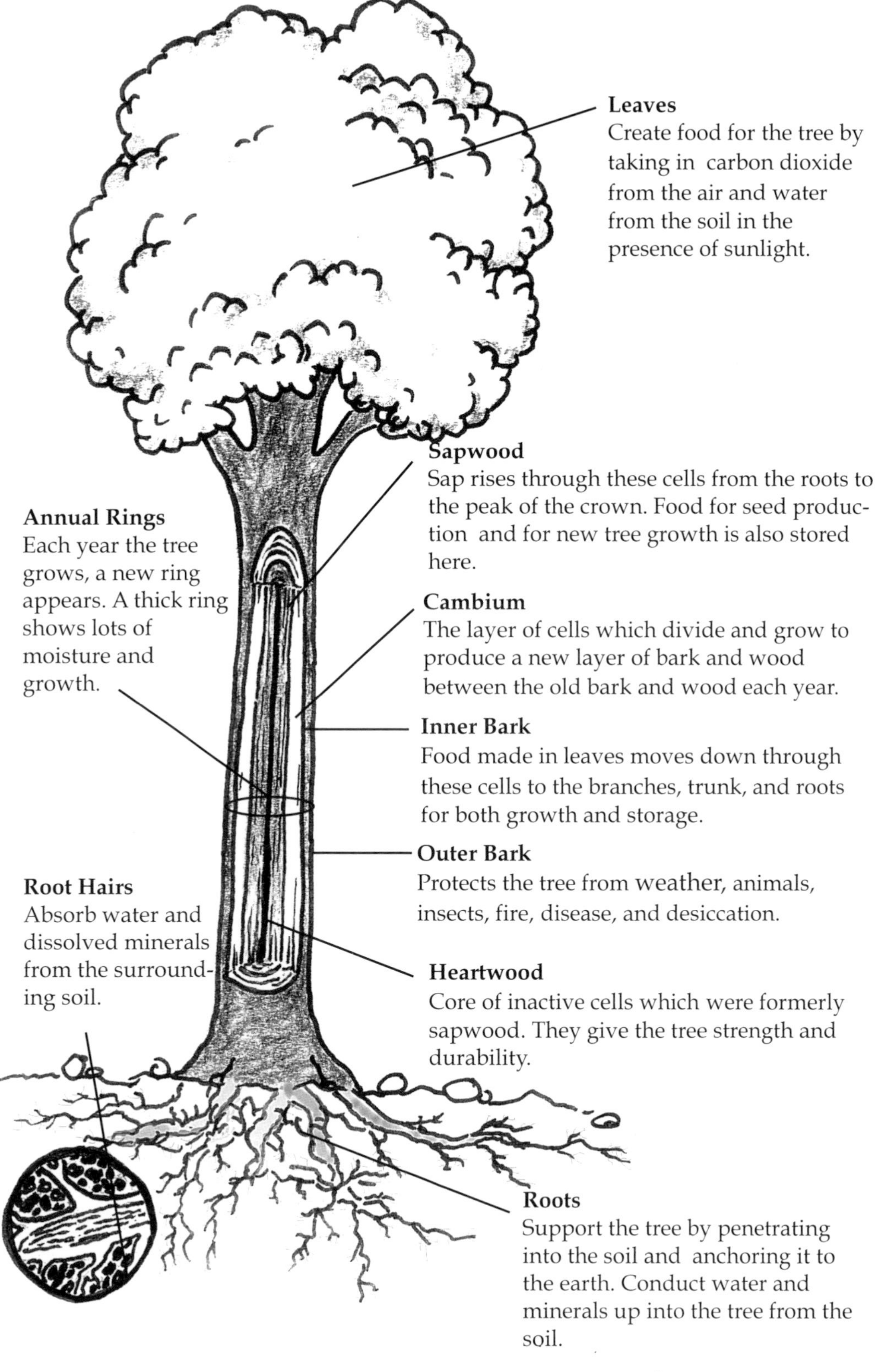

Leaves
Create food for the tree by taking in carbon dioxide from the air and water from the soil in the presence of sunlight.
Sapwood
Sap rises through these cells from the roots to the peak of the crown. Food for seed production and for new tree growth is also stored here.
Annual Rings
Each year the tree grows, a new ring appears. A thick ring shows lots of moisture and growth.
Cambium
The layer of cells which divide and grow to produce a new layer of bark and wood between the old bark and wood each year.
Inner Bark
Food made in leaves moves down through these cells to the branches, trunk, and roots for both growth and storage.
Outer Bark
Protects the tree from weather, animals, insects, fire, disease, and desiccation.
Root Hairs
Absorb water and dissolved minerals from the surrounding soil.
Heartwood
Core of inactive cells which were formerly sapwood. They give the tree strength and durability.
Roots
Support the tree by penetrating into the soil and anchoring it to the earth. Conduct water and minerals up into the tree from the soil.

13

Fourth-Grade Woodworking

by
David Mitchell

The child must work out of his or her own will, not by following commands. Thus, we can bring children to the point where they will carve and make various objects according to their own ideas.

– Rudolf Steiner

Beginnings are important times. When I have a class for the first time in the woodworking shop, I try to create a special, warm, and exciting atmosphere. The shop must be tidy and aesthetically decorated. Tools are visible on the wall, ordered, sharp and ready to be put to use. The different billets of wood are stored, and their fragrance permeates the space. The space should be such that when one enters, there is a desire to immediately start working

When the children of class four enter woodwork for the first time, I ask them to please sit in chairs I have placed in one straight line, and tell them we are going to start with a little game. They all put their hands behind their backs and close their eyes. I place an object, say a dry peach pit, in the hands of the child on the end, and then I have them pass it behind their backs without looking at it. They are asked to become as familiar with the object with their fingers and palms as they are able. When finished, I ask them to describe what their fingers experienced—using only adjectives. No nouns are allowed—the description is what is important. It is not important to know what it is! The children eagerly raise their hands and give descriptions such as: rough, pitted, oval, pointed at the ends, light, hard, and so on. Together they build up a picture of the object as determined by senses other than sight. Once a satisfactory picture is built up, I ask them what they think it is, and finally I show it to them and let them look at it for a few moments to validate their tactile experience. Then I pass other objects, perhaps a smooth small slab of rock maple, a piece of oak bark, a horse chestnut in its shell, an acorn, a roughly rasped piece of wood—and finally I conclude by passing a small carved wooden egg.

Through this activity the children are pulled out of their heads. They are asked to perceive with their sense of touch. They use different parts of their hands—the fingertips, the palm, the index finger and the thumb. Their hands become their eyes. We talk about the hand and notice that every finger can touch the thumb (opposability), and the entire hand can expand and contract into a fist (prehensility). The hand also allows us to do things like climbing, opening doors, sewing with a needle and thread, planting a garden, and building a house. We extol the wonders of the human hand as the class adds other things we can do. We conclude by observing how wonderful it is that our hands can make things for other people.

Next, I ask them to look around the workshop. All our tools are aesthetically displayed. I speak with them about the tools and tell them that they will be learning how to use all of them, and how each takes a special skill to master. Anticipation and eagerness is felt. Each tool is lovingly shown to them. The clamps and vices are explained; the ripsaw and crosscut saw are differentiated. I show them how a piece of wood cut with a sharp blade is smoother than a piece of wood sandpapered. They are allowed to smell the delicious aroma of our specially prepared beeswax-paste finish that we will be using to polish our finished projects.

Then I take a bolt of wood and an axe, and I split it in half and show them the grain. Carefully, I reduce a section down to a thin sliver. I then take a sawn cross-section which shows clearly the circular rings indicating the growing seasons. They learn to recognize when one season was rainy and supported growth (thick ring) and another season was dry and cloud covered (thin ring). Finally, we count the rings on a chunk of wood about the size of my upper arm, and the children are amazed to learn that the piece of wood is twice as old as they are. This helps build up a feeling of reverence for the materials we are going to work with. Such reverence is a key to awakening the moral sense for conservation and environmental care.

The children are told that high standards are set in the workshop. A project is only finished when it is scrutinized by both the student and the teacher and both agree that it has reached a satisfactory level of perfection.

In the pedagogical Oxford Course, Rudolf Steiner stressed the connection between handwork, practical arts, and art:

> *Let us take into account that the whole education and instruction touches the whole man. This can be done if the instruction comes out as a whole from the hearts of the teachers. It will become noticeable when the instruction flows from the soul element into the physical and practical. And this flowing into the physical and practical is the main concern of the Waldorf School. We try to let the children use their hands more and more. We work upward from the way in which the small child uses its hands in play to a certain artistic element, which is also taken out of the child itself. This is accomplished by beginning in the sixth grade with the artistic side. Many of these things belong to an earlier age, but we are forced to make compromises. We won't be able to attain the ideal until later. Then a nine-year-old will be able to do the things—also in the practical field—now done by the eleven- and twelve-year-olds. But these practical things are characterized by free work and inclusion of the artistic. The child must work out of its will, not by following commands. Thus, we can bring the children to the point where they will carve and make various objects according to their own ideas. . . .*

The atmosphere in the workshop is casual, and it is important to have warmth and humor so that the children feel relaxed, but care must be taken that they never become wild. I tell the children that we have no rules in the woodworking shop because they are unnecessary. They are now old enough to be able to use common sense, so that obviously we can have no running or horseplay around sharp objects because someone would get hurt. I then ask them to contribute what other commonsense observations we should follow in our woodworking shop. Finally, I ask them, "Don't you think that common sense is better than having a lot of rules?" They always agree and feel proud of the fact that they have helped to establish the parameters dictated by the space and activity for themselves.

It is important that the children actually begin their projects on the first day. Thus, some of what has been outlined above can be carried into the prologue to subsequent classes.

Now the class is ready to begin.

I tell the children that the first tool they will master is the most important tool of all. With it you can make almost anything, if you have patience enough. That tool is the knife. At this point they are shown a $3^1/_2$-inch sløyd knife from Scandinavia which is especially safe and practical for hand carving. I point out the different parts of the blade—the point, the edge, the tang, and the handle. I describe how one draws and pushes the blade from the butt of the edge toward the point in a slow, controlled gesture. Then I take a square of basswood and proceed to demonstrate. They watch as the wood curls away and drops off. After several strokes, I show them the curls and let them feel the softness and smoothness left by the blade cutting the basswood. The children first touch it with their fingers, and then I encourage a few to rub it against their cheeks. They exclaim in joy how smooth the wood is.

Then I show them how they must always carry and pass their knives—handle forward, waist-high, with the blade in the palm of the hand, edge up. I hand the knife to the end child and ask her to pass it on. As this proceeds, I correct and adjust, so that all children understand how they will walk with their knives.

Our first project is an egg carved from a rectangle of basswood. The egg necessitates an understanding of grain direction. Its completion exercises and trains both small and gross motor skills. Other projects can be little mice or a fish—the important thing is to have them create a convex shape. The children who finish quickly go on to carve a letter opener from purple lilac. Both projects are burnished, rubbed with a special oil mixture, and finally polished with beeswax.

I often tell a story, which continues onto the next class, to help the class focus on their work. I like to tell humorous stories like "Frederick the Mouse" or "Stan Bolovan the Dragon Tamer." The story takes several classes to complete, and the children are always eager to hear it resumed. The rule of thumb I developed was: stories permeate grades 4 to 5, while guided conversations permeate grades 6 to 8.

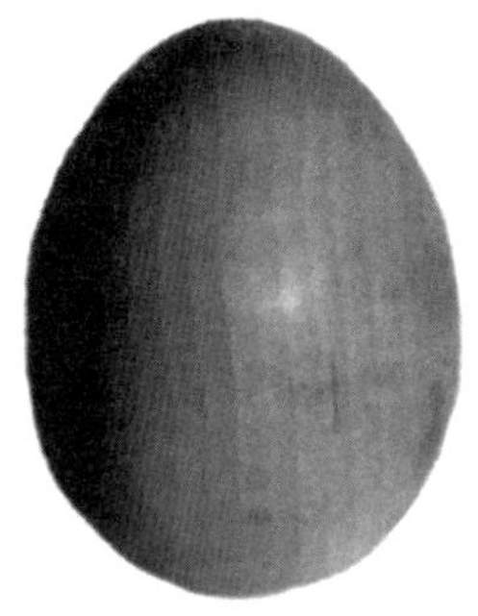

An egg is the first project. The convex shape teaches the student about grain direction.

Snake cut from a branch, sectioned, and using glued leather strips at joints for flexibility.

A recipe for a beeswax finish

Warm one cup of mineral oil in a saucepan over low heat, and melt a chunk of beeswax in it equal to about one-fifth or one-sixth the volume of the oil. (At high heat, there's a potential for fire. Be sure to keep the heat low, and consider using a double boiler.) As the wax begins to flake apart and dissolve, stir frequently. When the mixture is blended, add a capful of raw linseed oil, and then pour it into a used peanut can with a plastic lid to cool and solidify. To apply, rub in an excess of the soft paste with your fingers, let it dry a bit, then wipe it off with a soft non-lint rag. I have the children apply 3-4 coats and buff to a high polish. If you want to apply it as a liquid, you can reheat it.

14

Fifth-Grade Woodworking

by
David Mitchell

There is no objection if the children want to make cooking spoons. Let them do nothing foreign to their daily life, above all no luxury articles.

– Rudolf Steiner

The fifth graders hike out in the woods on their first day of woodworking. We search out different varieties of trees, observe how they grow, look at a leaf, compare it to the tree's crown, examine the underbrush—whether the soil is wet or sandy—and discuss the ecology of the forest. Next, we take a buck saw, fell and limb a particular tree, hoist it to our shoulders, and as a class we joyfully carry it back to the sawbucks outside our workshop. What easy work it is to carry the big tree when everyone puts a shoulder to it!

A theme for this year is concavity and working with natural timber. If we decide to make a box or a pencil or spoon holder, we select a four-inch diameter ash tree. We use ash because it holds onto its bark so nicely and gleams under a coat of varnish.

If we decide to make a birch piggy bank, we fell a four-inch diameter birch tree. With the bucksaw we each cut a five or six-inch bolt which we then plane, gouge out, and fashion into a piggybank. Holes are augured with a one-inch bit in a bit-and-brace. Legs, ears, and head are carved with a sløyd knife. We then go on to make individual spoons and scoops. Children who work quickly also make such diverse projects as a letter opener out of lilac, boomerangs, or small bowls.

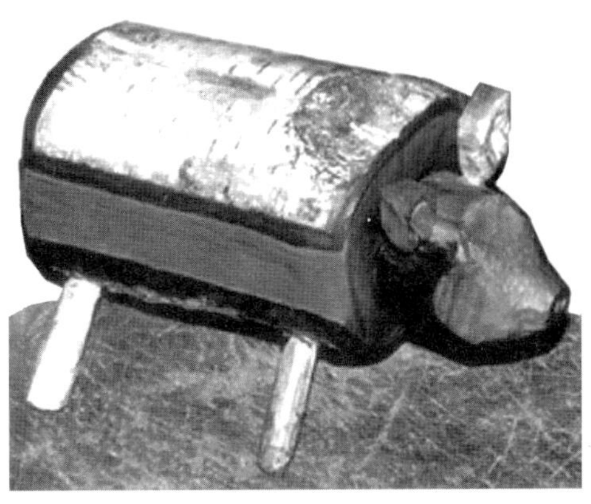

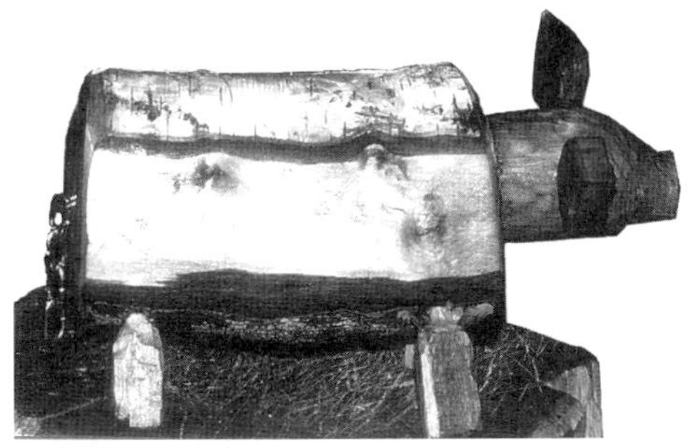

The emphasis is on using natural resources from the forest to make usable projects. The fifth graders want to discover and experience the surrounding world. For them it is good to come in contact with wood in its natural state and to use basic tools to transform it into practical objects. The artistic expression is focused on concave shapes at first. We add the convex shape afterward with the second project—a wooden spoon.

The children can discover the secrets and nature of the structure of wood on their own by observing and experimenting. Branches and logs are cut with the crosscut saw to the right length. The wood is split with a wedge and sledge hammer, an axe, or a froe. Planes, scrapers, glass, files, and sandpaper bring out the finish, and so on.

By splitting the wood lengthways, the grain keeps intact so that strong elastic pieces of wood are left. In ancient times such pieces were used for making tools, handles, primitive domiciles, the skeletons of boats, and other essential items.

Several pieces of different species (maple, lilac, oak, beech, walnut, mahogany, and others) are laid out on a bench. The children are reminded of the different qualities of the wood and how the grain makes different appearances. They are then allowed to select the wood of their choice.

On a piece of paper they trace the outline of their billet. With a ruler they draw a line down the middle and then carefully design their spoon on the paper with a pencil. After the design is approved by the teacher, they cut it out with scissors and trace it onto the billet.

The teacher places a pencil "X" in the center of the bowl portion of the spoon, helps them to clamp it tightly onto the table top, and has them select a gouge and mallet. All initial strokes are directed from the periphery toward the "X". Working around the bowl they slowly form a smooth concavity by putting aside the mallet and working with only their hands in carefully guided movements of the chisel.

Then they turn the spoon over, and the teacher makes another "X" on the side opposite the first at the deepest level of the concavity. Arrows are drawn from the "X" to the 360° periphery. The children then carefully follow the arrows, gouging away wood but leaving the "X" untouched. In this manner they create a convex shape which combines with the concave to form the bowl of the spoon. Riffler files and sandpaper complete the smoothing process. A saw is used to create kerfs at each side of the base of the bowl, and the handle is carefully split with a small axe. This provides a rough handle which is rasped to roundness with a bastard file. I have the students carefully use pieces of broken heavy glass (such as from an old coke bottle) to smooth the handle to a silky texture. Sandpaper will also work, if it is followed by wet and dry sandpaper and linseed oil. Finally, a beeswax finish is applied, and the spoon is hand polished.

The limb of an ash tree is drilled with a bit and brace and then hollowed with gouges. A one-inch slab is cut and made into a wedge so that it fits snuggly into the female shaped wedge formed in the bottom of the limb with a rasp. This primitive bowl is very functional and can store wooden spoons, pencils, or other objects. The outside is finished with spar varnish.

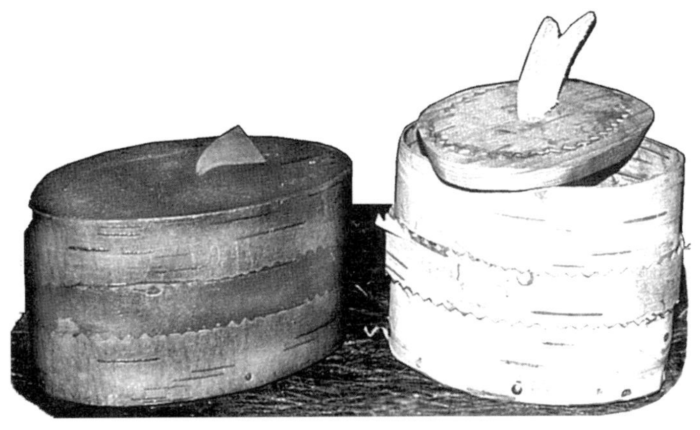

Birch bark boxes with an interior oval pine base and a leather tong on the lid can be an extra project for students who finish their spoons quickly.

15

Sixth-Grade Woodworking

by
David Mitchell

> *At the appropriate age, which occurs quite early in life, we let the children make their own toys. . . .Let them carve toys out of wood and thus combine their play with an artistic element. Actually, it corresponds to human nature itself if we gradually transmit playing into artistic formation and also into that practical formation of which I have spoken before. It is extraordinarily interesting that the artistic creativity of sculpturing is used by the children for the making of toys.*
>
> *Thus, we can transform the artistic element into arts and crafts. The children can learn to make simple tools, such as saws and knives as well as tools to be used by the cabinetmaker for his work. The boys and girls stand full of enthusiasm in our workshops. Full of enthusiasm, they include this fashioning of knives and saws and other tools in their schoolwork. And they are glad to be able to do these things, which can be utilized in life. In this way, all the instincts for life are stimulated. We see how, on the one hand, the sense for the practical; on the other hand, the sense for art is actually formed.*
>
> *Here a very essential guiding line has been developed: to gradually transfer the play of the child into artistic formation and the latter, in its turn, into practical formation.*
>
> – Rudolf Steiner

The sixth grade has begun to explore "cause and effect" in the science main lessons. This is a wonderful time to have the children design and make moveable toys.

In the autumn of 1920, Rudolf Steiner gave the following comments in regard to handicrafts, without reference to any specific grade, to the new handicrafts teacher, Max Wolffshügel:

> *It seems to me that, in doing handicrafts, we should always cultivate the artistic feeling, as a matter of course. We let the children do different things alternately and always finish them. Let them make not only useful objects, but also toys—good toys. It would be nice to let the children make a toy of two smiths moving towards each other; such things make the pupil skillful. They can use them as presents.*

There are many moveable toys that can be made. Each offers a different experience of "cause and effect" as well as of laws of physics, which they have been studying in their main lessons. Some of these projects are illustrated in this chapter.

Woodchoppers made from branches.

Owls wiggle their ears and flap their wings when the cord is pulled.

Steamroller constructed fromthe limbs of a fallen oak.

Push the plunger and the bird pecks at the corn on the stump.

I offered a limited choice of projects, so that the children could participate in selecting what they made.

Puppets made from branches and fishing line.

A woodpecker door-knocker to be hung on outside door.

Some children chose to design and shape a sailboat with keel out of a bolt of linden (basswood). They fashioned the entire vessel, sewed sails out of canvas, added lead ballast to the keel, and figured out the technology of making their rudder work. Others made a variety of moveable toys (see examples).

For a second project they could make hand-mirrors (purchase four-inch diameter beveled round mirrors), bowls, candle holders, lilac letter openers, carving boards, or wooden masks.

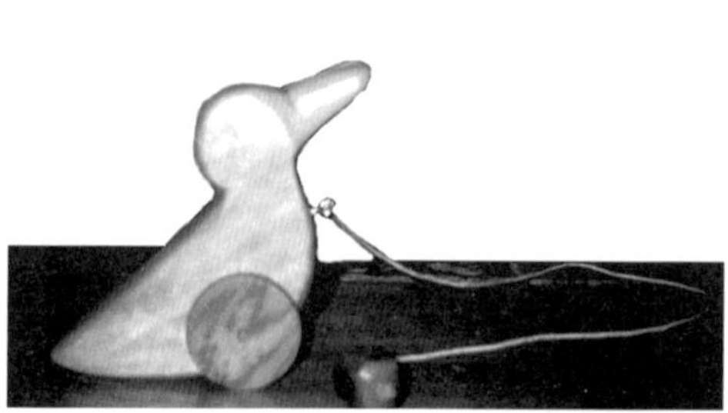

Pull animals with off center wheels to make interesting movement.

16

Seventh-Grade Practical Arts

by
David Mitchell

Flexible, agile fingers in childhood lead to mobile, creative thinking in adult life.
– Alstan L. Hegg

It is advisable to adopt a new approach in this class. At puberty the right mediums are wood, stone, and the metals. The puberty experience is one of death (the child dies, the adolescent is born), and one of the most powerful agents in overcoming these death forces is to allow and help the children to model and carve—to transform material by enlivening it through the forming power within their own spirit.

The seventh grade classes that I taught began the year by carving soapstone animals which they mounted on plaques or bases of hardwood. We were fortunate to have a soapstone quarry nearby where I was able to secure many rough pieces every year as a donation to the school. As I wrestled with underbrush and poison ivy to get the stone, I wondered if Waldorf teacher training had properly prepared me!

The students worked outdoors on large, chest-high stumps. Safety glasses were always worn as we rough-hewed the stones into various animal shapes with small axes purshased at the flea market. Using rasps, rifflers, hacksaw blades, and shurform tools, we brought out details and smoothness. The stones were finished by sanding them with progressive grades of wet-and-dry paper in a tub filled with water. A white froth would appear as a silky surface emerged.

The stones were given a quick clear lacquer spray, dried, and were then waxed and buffed to a high luster using our special beeswax paste.

For a second project, the faster students carved lilac letter openers, while others did woodburning, chip carving, or made a lidded box.

We also carved slabs of pine for woodblock printing and then used them to print on cloth and paper with various colored inks.

Finally, the class worked with copper. Some students did engraving to make copper/leather bookmarks while others did copper stamping and produced pictures of animals. Still others worked rhythmically chasing sheet copper in concave wooden forms, transforming the copper into simple bowls.

The first task was to set a compass to a $3^1/_2$-inch radius and then scribe a circle on a copper plate. Hand shears cut the circle exactly. The circumference was filed smooth with a flat file, using one-directional strokes, aimed away from the body. The copper was then placed in a concave depression in one of the two large stumps which stood proudly in our shop. Then, a hard leather mallet directed blow after blow in a rhythmical, even series starting on the outside and spiraling toward the center. The students experienced the copper becoming hard, and so we had to anneal it. The tapping of the hammers serenaded our ears, the smell of the quenched copper attacked our nostrils, and the gleam of the polished copper delighted our eyes. The senses were fully activated. Work was being accomplished.

When the bowl has its rough shape we switch tools by going to a vice which has, clamped within its jaws, a highly polished ball-post stake. We took a mirror-faced planishing hammer in our hands. Again the bowl was carefully hammered, one blow exactly next to the other, in a spiral, from the outside to the center. The facets formed threw the light, and the bowl took on a uniqueness from each student's individual technique. Finally, the bowl was hand polished, first with #0000 steel wool, then with copper polish and a soft cotton rag.

In addition, the children at this age should be taught the proper way to sharpen tools (knives, gouges, chisels, plane knives, and saws), and how to keep them sharp. They should learn how to use a slow, waterwheel, white grinding stone—either manual or electric. They should also learn to use a wet white Arkansas stone to keep the gouges sharp.

I also demonstrated how to properly set a saw with a saw set and how to use a triangular file to sharpen it. The students learned the purpose and design of a rip saw and a cross cut saw. We used a flat file to sharpen an axe, using a sweeping arc to keep the edge consistent. We used a stone to sharpen a draw knife and a small file to put an edge on a drill bit.

Puppets can be made in the seventh grade in conjunction with a puppet play written in English class where dialogue and quotations are being studied.

A carved frame backed by 1/4 birch ply makes a wonderful frame for postcards.

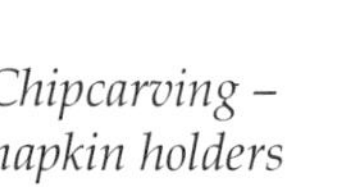

Chipcarving – napkin holders

Community Service

In the seventh and eighth grades I always included a community project as part of the practical arts curriculum. A portion of our shop time would be devoted to an altruistic service to the school or greater community. Over the years the seventh and eighth graders made benches for the schoolyard, helped build a woodshed, carved the school logo on a large solid plank of maple, made messenger ducks to be sold at the Christmas fair, and participated in building and outfitting a "gnome house" out of the hollow core of a dead apple tree.

The soft-handwork teacher loves to have buttons for projects, so we took branches from many types of trees, sawed them to size, carved them, sanded them and drilled holes. Then they were oiled and sanded once again and given as a gift to the soft-handwork teacher.

One year the parents were desperate for a small item for the Christmas Fair, so we set out to make dozens of these brightly painted message ducks. (Paper notes can be left in the duck's bill.) They were a great success, and the children were surprised at how many we could make in a production line.

A favorite community project was the Gnome House we would build to auction at the annual Pine Hill Waldorf School Christmas Fair. First, I would scour the woods for an old dead hollow apple tree. Then I would cut the trunk into two-foot sections. The children would use gouges to clean up the inside, and we would install a second floor with stairs and windows. Then we would make a soapstone stove with copper chimney pipes, beds, tables, wood chopping blocks with axes, rakes, shovels and anything that our imaginations could conjure up. A knitted family of gnomes with a baby in a cradle would complete the project.

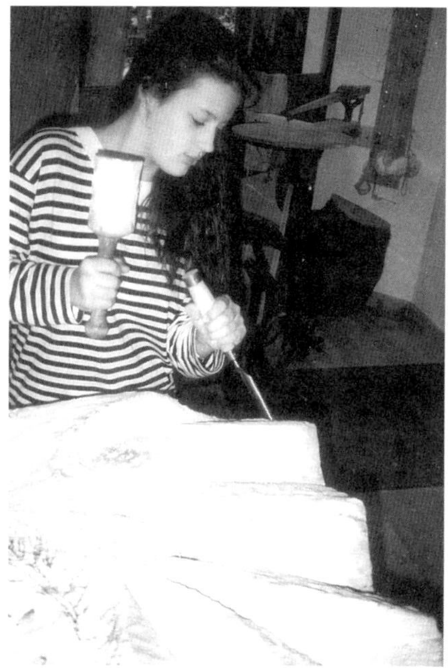

The faculty requested that we have a large copy of the Pine Hill Waldorf School logo carved and placed in the front lobby of the school, so we took a 5-inch thick slab of Rock Maple and used gouges to group carve the project. The class worked in groups of four. A paper varnished to the back identified all of the carvers.

17

Eighth-Grade Woodworking

by
David Mitchell

The quality of the world we live in is determined not only by what we perceive, but also by what we fail to perceive.

– Owen Barfield

The eighth grade is a time for precision work. The accurate measuring and sawing of a hinged, dovetailed box is a project that will challenge both boys and girls. Some of the boxes were designed specifically as jewelry boxes, while others were for tools or for music tapes. It is important that the students have a purpose for their boxes so their thinking will be incorporated in unique designs.

It is necessary to have a dovetail template and several backsaws. I also preferred wooden carpenter rulers. The wood was pre-sawn to width, and the students sawed it to length. Some were allowed to have friction fitted tops with the edges routed in, but I encouraged everyone to "set in" brass hinges. In some cases we made wooden hinges with dowel pins.

We made three-legged stools with the legs wedged in place in a "pin and hole" joint, and the chair was carved into a concave comfortable form with gouges and a spokeshave. The stool used no metal or glue and was totally constructed out of wood. Those students who wanted could make a small table instead of a stool, but the table top had to be solid and not made out of bits and pieces joined together.

The students were taught the use of spokeshaves, drawknives, and the block plane to plane the edges of the legs and even round off edges, and for the smoothing of the tabletop. They were taught the placing and cleaning of the plane. They also were acquainted with the sliding bevel and mandrel.

Prior to starting construction, the students were asked to make a simple work drawing and materials list. This insured that they thought through the project before beginning. The teacher should always strive to make sure that beauty and practicality (efficiency) coincide in the construction of the stool or table.

Other projects for the eighth grade included the making of puzzles in slide-top boxes. These consisted of paintings from fairy tales on $^1/_4$-inch birch plywood. We had a wonderful floor-pedal band saw to cut the puzzle patterns. These were placed in flat boxes with slide-top lids.

The students would carve elaborate reliefs of animals or scenes from nature in $1^1/_4$-inch thick slabs of sugar maple, or they could make hand mirrors out of various pieces of fruitwood.

Through the teacher's guidance, a child's proper attention to detail in practical skills during elementary school can metamorphose into a teenager's intellectual dexterity. In the early years of Waldorf education, work is developed as an outgrowth of play. In these primary years the teacher sets the foundation for the high school. Students should leave the middle school with a craving to know, an insatiable curiosity about everything that goes on around them, such that they can convert this deep interest into still further knowledge.

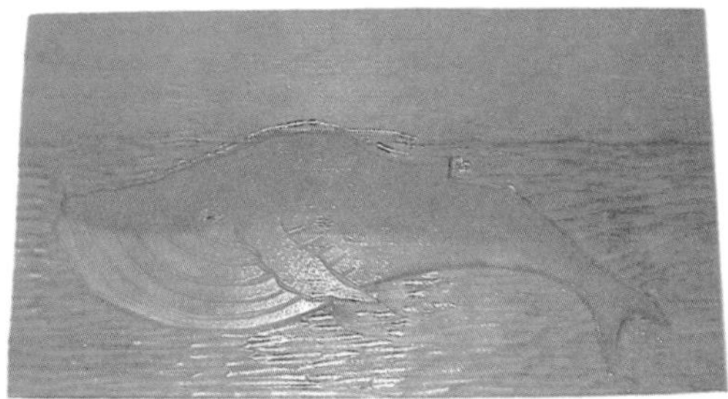

Relief carving of a Right Whale.

Motif #1 in Rockport, MA

Examples of carved boxes.

Applying a Finish

There are two basic groups of finishes:

1. Those which *penetrate the surface,* such as linseed oil, tung oil, and Danish oil.

The penetrating oils are the easiest to use, can be applied with a rag, and penetrate the surface pores of the wood and then harden. They can be buffed to a soft dull sheen, and they allow the natural grain to show through.

Tung oil, extracted from the nut of the Chinese tung tree dries to a hard film. When using tung oil, first saturate the wood and keep it moist for ten minutes or more. Then wipe it in with a soft cloth, allow to dry, then apply a second coat rubbing with the grain. Wait twenty-four hours and then rub another coat on, using #0000 steel wool between coats. Usually three coats are needed to achieve a low sheen and protective finish.

A polymerized oil is an oil which has been heat-treated. This oil absorbs oxygen from the air and hardens best.

Linseed oil, a dark, full-bodied oil, comes from the flax plant and is the base for traditional oil paints. Boiled linseed oil is the best to use because of its improved drying capabilities. Linseed oil is not very durable or moisture resistant.

2. The *surface finishes* such as varnish, shellac, lacquer, and polyurethane.

The surface finishes must be applied carefully with a brush or by spraying. They readily build up a protective coat which sits like a blanket on the surface of the wood. Consisting, for the most part, of resins, they are hard and durable. Most protect the wood from moisture, and they can give a brilliant sheen.

Lacquer, varnish, and polyurethane require care in application, but a hard surface is achieved. Light sanding is required between coats, and you must use a "tack cloth" to remove dust before applying the next coat.

Preferred finishes

After years of experimenting, I developed a fondness for a finish which was a combination of the two above. The formula is:

1/3 polyurethane, 1/3 tung oil, 1/3 boiled linseed oil,
plus a small amount of mineral spirits

The combinations above create a penetrating finish which enriches the tone of the wood, provides a durable, attractive, satin-sheen finish that can easily be rubbed into the wood. After it dries, I often then apply beeswax which can be polished to a warm sheen with a lint-free cotton cloth.

Another fine finish uses shellac and is called "French polish." Shellac is the resinous secretion from Thailand's Coccus Lacca bug. It has been used in woodworking for over 4,000 years, has excellent adhesive properties, and can be polished to a high gloss or rubbed out to a satin or flat sheen as desired.

Follow the steps outlined below:

1. Apply a base coat on your project by reducing a three-pound cut of shellac in half by adding an equal amount of denatured alcohol. Use a brush to apply the shellac to the wood, and ensure that you apply a good, even coat over the surface. This first thin coat will dry very quickly under most conditions.

2. Once the first coat of shellac is dry, apply a second coat. When this is dry, apply the third coat. After you have added all three coats, allow the shellac to dry for at least 12 hours. Then use 600 wet/dry sandpaper to smooth out the shellac. Wipe off the sanding dust with a tack cloth.

The base coat for the French polish is now prepared.

3. Now mix up the French polish using the $1^1/_2$-pound cut shellac that was used to create the base coat above. Pour it into a flat open pan such as an old pie pan.

Take a soft, lint-free cloth—such as cheesecloth—and fold it into a ball (called the "pad"). In the center of the pad place a full tablespoon or two of softened beeswax paste. Now dip the pad into the shellac so that it becomes moist, but not dripping, with shellac. Tap the pad in the palm of your hand in order to shake off excess shellac. The aim is to make sure that the entire front of the pad is damp. It is wise to wear rubber gloves; otherwise, your hands will get very sticky!

4. Work the pad swiftly onto your project, as if you were shining shoes, slapping the pad to the wood and off again. If you stop too long you will dissolve the base coat! As you "slap," slide the pad across the wood's surface and then take off again, working from left to right and then from right to left, overlapping each stroke as you apply it. Practice will help you perfect your technique. Slowly work from the bottom to the top and then start at the bottom again, ensuring that you have enough shellac on the pad so that the strokes are uniform. You can add a little lemon oil or cream polish to the pad to help make it slide easier, if the beeswax hasn't already done this.

5. Once you are satisfied with the wood's finish place the pad in a jar and seal the lid tightly so it will not dry out and can be used again. Allow the shellac to dry for at least a couple of hours and then take out the pad again. Add denatured alcohol to the pad and tap it in the palm of your hand to disperse the alcohol to the front of the pad. Then lightly pad over the wood's surface again. This process is known as "spiriting out" and serves to remove the oil as well as further evening out the shellac finish.

18

The Therapeutic Aspects of Handwork

by
Bonnie River

The secret of education lies in respecting the pupil.
– Ralph Waldo Emerson

A three-month-old baby lies on her back contentedly cooing and gurgling as she waves her hands, fanning her fingers before her eyes. She stretches out her arm as if to reach for something, her head turns toward her outstretched arm, and her eyes search for the tiny palm moving in the space to her side. She balls her fist and pulls it toward her mouth, as if to taste of the light grasped in that outward movement. As her fingers curl back out of the fist into an outstretched fan, she again makes many sounds of pleasure.

We have known for some time now that there is an active, direct connection between the articulated movements of the fingers and the articulation of the sounds of speech. Now research is elucidating a reciprocal relationship between the development of intelligence and eye-hand coordination. In his book entitled ***The Hand,*** Frank Wilson, M.D., a neurologist and the medical director of the Department of Medicine, University of California, San Francisco, states:

> *I would argue that any theory of human intelligence which ignores the interdependence of the hand and brain function, the historic origins of that relationship, or the impact of that history on the developmental dynamics in modern humans, is grossly misleading and sterile.*

The joining of the eye and the hand involves a complex hierarchy of learned tasks. As the child progresses up the ladder of coordinated functions, she will learn to inwardly track where each hand is in relation to the midline, to the root of the shoulder, the other hand, the mouth, even the foot and the eyes. These complicated movements serve to form an inner map of coordinates which orient any object in three-dimensional space.

Before there can be independent finger use, the child must have learned to use her arm to guide the hand into the range of vision, and the hand must orient to grasp an object and mold itself to the shape of the object. When these tasks are complete, a child is prepared to receive all the visual-spatial information she will experience when coming to upright.

The senses of touch and sight become synthesized through the explorations of the eye and the hand working in unison. The young child begins her coordination of these senses by orienting toward an object of interest. Through continuous and repetitive efforts to bring an object to vision, the child's movements become more and more fluid; thus, the sense of self-movement (proprioception) is fostered toward synthesis with the other two.

The coordination of eye, hand, and bodily movement begins in babyhood and continues throughout all of life. The refinement of the senses in their unique relationship to one another is an individual's life signature in the gifts she brings forth to share with her fellow humans.

As more and more research emerges which elucidates the importance of working with our hands, questions arise with regard to the nature of this work. To what degree does interest in what the hand is doing affect the actual acquisition of a skill? How do different types of skills affect intelligence and learning? Some correlates to these questions also beg to be queried. Is there a difference between our "punch button" technology, i.e., keyboard writing, breadmaking machines, and the like, and the skills acquired while, for example, kneading bread, knitting, or writing in cursive? To this Dr. Wilson states:

> *. . . When personal desire prompts anyone to learn to do something well with the hands, an extremely complicated process is initiated that endows the work with a powerful emotional charge. People are changed, significantly and irreversibly, it seems, when movement, thought, and feeling fuse during the active, long-term pursuit of personal goals.*

Another researcher of the mid-nineteenth century, Sir Charles Bell, a Scottish surgeon, anatomist, and contemporary of Darwin, wrote a treatise entitled ***The Hand, Its Mechanism and Vital Endowments, as Evincing Design***. In this work, he finds that no serious study and history of human development can ignore the central importance of the hand in meaningful activity.

Implicit in Rudolf Steiner's works on spiritual physiology is an imagination that the human organs of articulation are a microcosm of the entire bodily structure. The entire physical body is the spoken "word" of the hierarchies. Each part of the physical body was created out of tones of the cosmic world. Movement, thus, becomes the "word" on earth and metamorphoses to thought-filled sentences.

Many studies have been done of the tones sounded in the muscle and nerve activity, as reflected in the brain. In the field of sensory integration, descriptive phrases for the action of the muscles reflect a sense of musicality sounding through the body. A person can have a well-toned, flat toned (hypotonic), or sharp toned (hypertonic) muscle system. Interestingly, children with physical handicaps nearly always have muscle tone difficulties and have speech patterns which reflect these conditions.

Dr. Alfred Bauer, who developed Chirophonetics, an anthroposophical approach to speech and other disorders of incarnation, bases this work on a practitioner's ability to recapitulate the sounds and rhythms of speech through a touching of the hand (light stroking) upon the body of another. In this approach the practitioner can experience the relaxing of a cramped muscle and sense a flow returning or coming to the patient's speech organization. Here, the hand makes movements which activate the memory of the movements of the hierarchies in speech. Again, the senses of word and thought are seen as intimately connected to the hand in movement.

Today many schools are sensing the wisdom implicit in the Waldorf handwork curriculum. For example, teachers notice that tightly strung knitting stitches are also reflected in cramped handwriting and an anxious soul-stance toward life. One can see how handwork can become a force in healing when the teacher observes and guides the students appropriately. Additionally, handwork can serve to help remediate when the healthy toning between the child and the environment calls for such intervention.

Handwork strongly involves the relationship between the will (doing activity) and the feeling-life of the student, and, yet, one notices that the capacity for clear speech is enlivened through such activity, also. Speech, or the sense of language, is often named as the capacity that defines being human. Language is seen as evidence of intelligence.

Neuropsychologists are ever more aware that the brain's capacity to reflect accurate information and enable the individual to connect inner experience and outer world phenomena grows with the interdependent use of the visual, tactile, and proprioceptive systems. This reflective ability, called "concept formation," is dependent upon the use of the hand in gesture along with the acquisition of language. The Russian linguist Vigotsky theorized:

> *Well-developed thought arises as the verbal behavior of the child undergoes a long metamorphosis during which words, which were originally object attributes, come increasingly to be manipulated and combined, just as real objects are manipulated and combined by the child.*

If one considers what Vigotsky is stating, in light of handwork, one can conclude that as the hand works to combine and form what has been imagined, the brain centers for the development of a refined sense of language arts are enhanced.

As an educator, I am aware of the morphology of the sense of sequence and the usage of appropriate verb tense to indicate timing of actions. If a child is able to sequence a movement pattern, it is because they have "entered into" the movement through the faculty of visualization. This imaginative capability requires an inner sense of space in which processes unfold in time. Through repeated movements, the child is able to establish time within space. This ability is the foundation of, for example, reading comprehension, expository writing, or working math processes.

How exactly can space and time come into play through the use of the hands? This is the mystery of the at once opposing and collaborating use of the left and right hands. In general, if a child uses the right hand for initiating and articulating activities, then the left hand is in the position of support. This support position involves a visual-spatial sense of the object being held. Through the sense of the wholeness of the object (the space component), the analytical, functionary right hand can act in a timed sequence to transform the spatial object. Picture, if you will, the hand that holds a dish while the other hand acts upon that dish to clean it. Thus, the spatial object is transformed through sequenced movements of hands working in reciprocal relationship to one another.

If one could slip inside the neural pathways and sense the immense amount of movement coursing along and crossing back and forth across the corpus callosum as a person is executing planned movements, one would wonder at the process of establishing these pathways from one hemisphere of the brain to the other. It begs the question: "Does the joining of the left and right hemispheres of the brain depend on bodily movement?" I would not postulate that all brain efficiency is dependent upon motor planning. However, much research points to a direct relationship between developmental and hierarchical movements and brain efficiency or plasticity.

When a child is trying to remember how a word is spelled, she is searching for the visual form of the word in one hemisphere and must transfer this form onto paper or into sound using other areas of the brain. This involves neurotransmission through nerve pathways which traverse back and forth across the hemispheres matrixing information through many interrelated brain centers.

These neural pathways must be "exercised" or used repeatedly in order for them to attain efficiency. They are likened to "electrical lines" which, unless insulated, will short-circuit. The insulation, called myelin, grows as a result of repeated use. Thus, one could say that through activity, the brain's capacity to repeat and remember an activity is enhanced. Herein is a secret of the astral body imprinting upon the etheric; thus, memory is born.

The use of the hands involves the "crowning" point of the entire movement system. Posture must be stabilized in order for the child to articulate movements through the sternum across the clavicle, around the joints, down the long bones of the arm to reach the tiny bones and ligaments of the wrist and fingers. This sequence of movements is reflected in the brain, and the matrix for sequential learning is established or enhanced.

Researchers in the field of neuropsychology of learning mention one important factor in the process of eye and hand connection. It has been found that meaningful activity fosters stability and virtuosity in brain function. A person traveling through a foreign land, devoid of the capacity to speak the language, is able to communicate through gesture, posture, and facial expressions. This is possible because meanings (concepts laden with feelings) are universal.

When children are tested for learning capacities and achievement, and when the testing instrument itself has no meaning to the child, the examiner invariably mentions this fact. It is known that performance is lower when the activity has no intrinsic meaning to the test taker.

Imagine the handwork experience: visualizing your project, choosing the materials, colors, size, shape, and so forth, and knowing that what you are about to make is something useful and meaningful in the world. With the urge to create something meaningful, the imagination of the finished work, and the sequential and carefully planned movements, one has constellated all that is necessary for the eye and hand to lovingly create that which the mind will joyfully reflect. At the same time the individual's thinking is becoming both exercised and strengthened.

19

In Reverence for the Human Hand

by
Elizabeth Auer

He who works with his hands is a laborer.
He who works with his hands and head is a crasftsman.
He who works with his hands, head, and heart is an artist.
– St. Francis of Assisi

Two human hands reach out toward each other. The fingers feel the other's skin, whole hand feels the strength of the handshake. As the two hands meet, one pair of eyes look into the other, words are spoken, a beginning is taking place in the heart.

The human hand is built on the number five with a total of twenty-seven bones. From the narrow wrist it radiates outward as an extension of our humanity reaching out into the world.

Forming a unit with the arm, it begins with the humerus as a single bone, changing to the radius and ulna as a twosome, becoming the first three wrist bones, followed by four more wrist bones, and finally culminating in the five carpals. The muscles of the shoulder move the upper arm in relation to the body, while those in the upper arm move the forearm by bending or straightening the elbow. The muscles in the forearm work the hand bones in the palm and some of the finger bones. Besides moving in relation to the humerus, to bend the elbow, the forearm bones, the radius, and the ulna also move on each other, at their upper and lower ends. They rotate to swivel over each other in a movement that twists the wrist so that the palm faces down—called pronation.

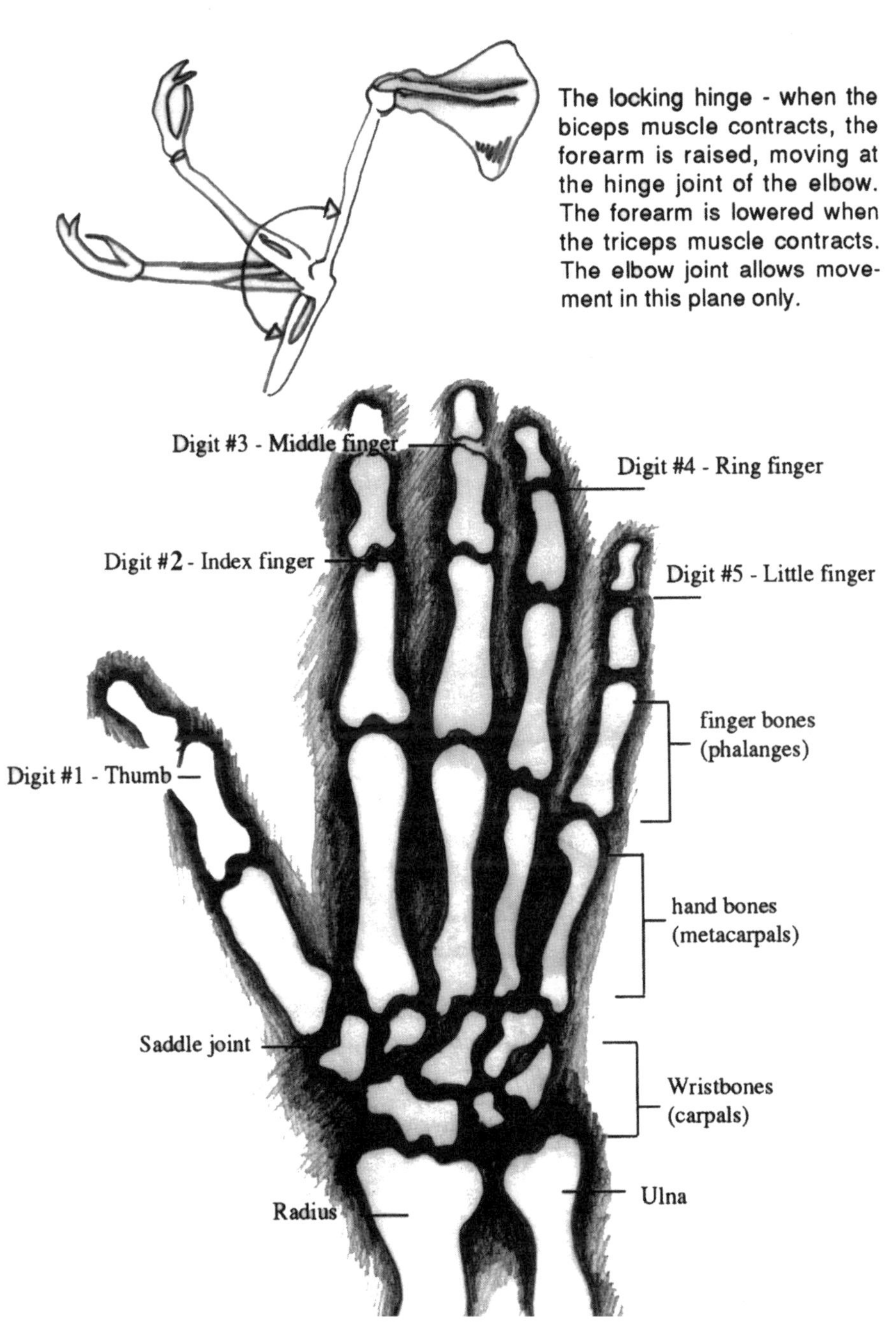
The locking hinge - when the biceps muscle contracts, the forearm is raised, moving at the hinge joint of the elbow. The forearm is lowered when the triceps muscle contracts. The elbow joint allows movement in this plane only.
Digit #3 - Middle finger
Digit #4 - Ring finger
Digit #2 - Index finger
Digit #5 - Little finger
finger bones (phalanges)
Digit #1 - Thumb
hand bones (metacarpals)
Saddle joint
Wristbones (carpals)
Ulna
Radius

The wrist is a complex joint with eight bones, allowing considerable flexibility. The eight bones are wrapped in strong supporting ligaments. Each bone moves on all its neighbors. The bones are made of cartilage in babies, turning to bone gradually during childhood. They provide anchorage for the small muscles that help to move the thumb and fingers.

The human hand is distinguished by the position of its extremely mobile thumb. The long metacarpal bones of the thumb are "hidden" in the palm of the hand. At the base of the first metacarpal is a very mobile saddle joint which allows the thumb to bend in two planes. The thumb can touch each fingertip in turn. This precision grip is the basis of the human hand's dexterity.

A complex network of nerves accompany the bones and muscles and in the hand radiate outward into the fingers. They are the threads from the spinal cord that bring all the components together so that the movement can take place, along with the blood flowing through the veins bringing oxygen from the heart. A rich network of nerves fills the fingertips. In the movement and interaction they make with substances that they are forming, the creative form-building capacities of the muscles are being strengthened. The fingers become nimble, the powers of thinking grow to develop nimble minds; with the flow of the blood they create stirrings within the heart.

The sand is wet from the waves crashing onto the beach. Young hands are busy with shovel and bucket, packing the wet particles more and more tightly together. The bucket is turned upside down with a flick of the wrists and quickly placed on the flat surface. The first form has been placed, followed by numerous others, patted and shaped this way and that, placed next to and on top of each other. Tunnels are dug, the fingers working busily as excavators, pushing and scooping, creating hollow, empty spaces.

The beeswax lies cold, stiff, and shapeless. A lump of golden yellow is picked out from among the many colors and begins slowly to become permeated with warmth flowing from the palm of the hand, giving it flexibility and malleability. The fingers warm the beeswax through and through working together in unison, pressing up and down, back and forwards; the body of a lion emerges, the head, the legs, the tail.

So the forming power of the human spirit dawns in the young life, a life that is growing and forming itself, a young life that inwardly imitates movement that flows as formative force into the hands—a constructive activity, bringing the blood and life forces into thorough movement in the fingertips.

Wool—a gift from the sheep when shorn. Washed in water, teased and stretched. The counter motion of two hands carding back and forth, creating out of fibrous chaos a singularity of direction. Stretching and pulling, twirling and twisting, the innumerable fibers join forces into ever lengthening yarn.

The thumb and forefinger draw close together, coming to rest and bearing down on both sides of a flower petal. With a quick motion of the wrist the petal is plucked off from the stem of the blossom; goldenrod, pokeberries, apple twigs, beechnuts, oak galls, and lichens are scraped from bark. Collected in a stone vessel, the gifts from the plant world are pounded by hand with strong, vigorous, rhythmic activity, pressing hard and deep into the hollow shape of the resistant, hard stone. The tiny treasures of flower color are mixed with water and heat to bring the rainbow into the fibers.

The thumb and the forefinger adapt themselves this time to holding a nail, poised for the hammer in the other hand to strike the first blow. The eye is watchful as again and again the hammer bears down and finds its way down to the head of the nail. Two hands are working as companions and friends, each helping and balancing out the other.

The nails are waiting in two opposite rows to receive the warp. The fingers curl around the yarn ever so lightly, and as the hand moves up and down, bending the yarn around the nails, the yarn glides through the curled over, hollow space created by the fingers. The warp now awaits the weft. In and out, over and under, the fingers move in dialogue with one another, weaving in the golden rod yellow and the pokeberry purple through the tightly stretched warp. The eye watches carefully to see that the fingers respect each individual, stretched piece of yarn, that the yarn going across goes rhythmically under and over and that the edges of the warp are growing regularly and straight. At intervals the rhythm changes and the yarn rests for a moment while the four fingers of each hand in a unified motion pull down the rows of the weft, so that they fit snugly next to each other.

Animal, plant, stone, and water are gifts for human hands to transform in turn into gifts to give to other human hands to hold, to behold, to feel, to cherish.

Wood—a picture of the mineral world drawn up into the sphere of a plant, possessing the pureness of the plant yet the hardness of the mineral. It is a picture of the overcoming of the hardness of substance.

A pencil moves over the surface and creates a central line down the length. It guides the eye as a symmetrical shape is drawn, a form drawing marking the beginning of the spoon. One hand holds the gouge, feeling and seeing its way ahead, the guiding force in the partnership. The other hand holds the mallet, bearing down on the handle of the gouge, providing the will and intention in movement to create the hollow concave bowl that forms the cup. Rhythmically the hard substance is removed; a transformation is taking place. The rasp is held in both hands to shape the handle, one giving the moving force and the other complementing, balancing the activity, guiding the directions of movement. The eye has been looking on, observing each movement, the mind making constant judgments and numerous minute decisions as to how to proceed with each step, searching for the symmetry. The head and the hands are working together—and all of it taking place right in front of the region of the body where the heart is held enclosed by the lungs which breathe in and out, giving life forces to the whole.

Marble—a white, earthly substance, the mineral in its hard, yet at times brittle and delicate form. In the one hand the chisel with its fine point moves around and explores the surface, receiving the force from the mallet in the other hand, that makes it possible for small pieces to break off and fall away. Slowly and gradually the hidden, hitherto unknown form emerges.

A sense of form is awakening from within; a sense of beauty reaches out to the world of stone, plant, animal, and man. Human thinking, feeling and willing express themselves in the working together of hands, head, and heart.

Elizabeth Auer teaches clay modeling, stone and wood carving, stained glass, and metal work at the Pine Hill Waldorf School in New Hampshire.

Part 2
The Waldorf High School

High school student tending the fire in a blacksmith forge.

20

Practical Arts and the Adolescent

by
David Mitchell

We want to feel the chair's beauty when we sit in it.
– Rudolf Steiner

Idealism is kept alive in the high school curriculum when all the subjects are centered around the human being. A life philosophy is evolved where science, art, and religion are not artificially separated; the qualitative as well as the quantitative experience are cultivated. When the students study the computer, they are also learning something about themselves. The same is true in the crafts.

Steiner identified two great obstacles which face adolescents, and he offered suggestions as to how a curriculum could be formulated to assist the youth in meeting them. The first is sexual lust, which can be met by keeping them busy with meaningful tasks, by encouraging them to strive for beauty, and by keeping their hands busy with such subjects as handwork, jewelry making, blacksmithing, stone sculpture, woodcarving, and joinery.

The second danger is the lust for power. To keep them from succumbing to this, the teachers and parents must continually inspire the teenager's thinking. Great ideas and moral thoughts must be brought to them. Their intellect must be kept moving and altruism encouraged.

The capacity for conceptual thought lies on a higher level of cognitive development. The process of abstraction can be exercised by having the students analyze their own work. The method of examining why a piece of copper became too thin in a particular area, or why a joint of a compound dovetail didn't fit lends itself to such mental evaluation.

A key to the education of adolescents is to provide activities which focus their will energy. Modern society has not provided teenagers with enough to do! Up to this point in their lives almost everything has been done for them, so they "hang" out. They take on a "slumping attitude" and become a "hormonal hazard." When their will is directed by tasks they do in the practical arts, they become different people. They become more integrated into life and more fully incarnated onto the earth.

The puberty experience is often refered to as a kind of death during which childhood ends and adolescence begins. Rudolf Steiner described it as a "gentle sprinkling of pain that never goes away." Humor and patience are antidotes, and becoming engaged with one's hands becomes an active outlet allowing one to forget onself. This adolescent time is one where aesthetics and form are needed to create life harmony.

It's the task of the teacher to be able to guide the adolescents through their painful introspection, to help them let go of their own stuck intentions, and help them to recognize what each medium has to present from within itself. The students have to go through a metamorphosis of their own intentions and allow themselves to work in partnership with the material, be it stone or wood. This process is learned through repetition. When the students sculpt a human head in clay in the ninth grade and then have to repeat it in stone in the twelfth grade, they will experience a new awakening.

The practical arts provide the opportunity for the student to carve, model, and forge—to transform materials through the force of their will and to enliven them with the power of their own spirit.

Each of the crafts calls upon a development of different capacities. Wood requires "listening" to the possibilities of the material. When using a blockplane, the craftsman develops a unity with the board. Woodworking is directed toward our realm of *feeling*. We leave our self-concern and live into the activity.

With stone we need to organize our *will* activity. The stonecarver is called upon to work with the grain and texture of each unique piece of stone. He has to be able to "see" into the stone and its possibilities. The stonecarver demonstrates his *will* with point and hammer. We actively link all our concentration with our actions.

The metalworker has to work primarily with *thinking*. It is not strength which makes a good blacksmith, but, rather, precise blows of the hammer. Every beat of the smith must be to exactly the right point—the point is the image of the thought in the deed. Exact, thought-through construction drawings and precisely built jigs are at the genesis of almost every project. Our thinking and our will become syncronized.

Once the student has been connected to the subject through his feeling for it, and awakened in his thought life, then the knowledge can flow into his will, into his active deeds. A Chinese proverb states the following:

When I hear — I forget
When I see — I remember
When I do — I understand

To be absorbed in creative activity is the real joy of life. The creative process gives rise to, rather than depletes, energy. One can feel relaxed, in control, at peace, and in harmony. In carving and modeling, the student can find an excellent outlet for his or her creative energies. It is difficult, if not impossible, to be absorbed in pursuing a meaningful goal and to be depressed at the same time.

Self-observation, self-evaluation, and the capacity to take on responsibility are characteristics of personal growth. Skill learned in the crafts becomes the development of practical consciousness. This practical consciousness has its genesis in an increased power of observation.

The following chapters demonstrate how this can be realized during the high school years.

High school students building a storage barn using post and beam construction.
–photo by Ed Edelstein

21

The Curriculum

by
David Mitchell

In a Waldorf high school you may find such practical courses as house building, carving, basket weaving, spinning, dyeing, bookbinding, sewing with both treadle and electric machines, locksmithing, papermaking, shoemaking, surveying, soap making, automobile mechanics, batik, enameling, calligraphy, stained-glass making, stone carving, furniture making, pottery, and jewelry making. All students participate in phases of these courses, and as they progress through the school, some students might focus on one craft to develop an expertise in it.

Adolescence is a time when development is individualized. Teenagers come into different stages in a very individual way based on their own body chemistry, so it's hard to classify them. But, generally, in the sophomore summer one notices a real transition taking place. The bookbinding and box-making the students do in the eleventh grade are a preparation for allowing the thinking to be released in quite a new way. At this age self-sufficiency and self-reliance can be observed in the clarity of their thinking.

Each school, out of its own demographics, brings craftsmen and craftswomen of competence into its program. There might be a school that has the good fortune to have a locksmith who can really develop the locksmithing in the upper high school years. This is a wonderful craft which really allows thinking to be visible in terms of the interrelationship of the mechanical components of the lock.

A school might have a shoemaker, and each student can be involved with a lathe and be making his or her own shoes. Other schools may have a blacksmith, and metallurgy can be developed. Another school may have a jeweler and the ability to work with stone and wire of gold and silver formed into intricate and delicate patterns.

Another school may be fortunate to have a textile worker who really is an expert in batik. This is probably one of the most beloved of crafts in Waldorf schools. The wonderful patterns that can come out of batik on clothing are loved by the students. A very important task is to find a seamstress who can guide the students to sew the costumes for plays.

The Toronto Waldorf School has built many canoes and kayaks as part of its woodworking curriculum. I know another school that has built musical instruments of a high quality.

Other schools have developed house building. They have actually had their students construct a post and beam house all the way from milling the lumber at the sawmill to going right into the wiring and plumbing. This "spec" house was sold, and the funds invested in the next project. They reconstructed individual rooms as well as an entire building on campus. There are other schools that have taken other crafts and really developed them to a high skill level. The students were seen more as apprentices who learned how to do something at the level of the perfection of the craftsman.

There is a discipline that comes from such work. It is interesting how different schools have different expressions, but the main intention is that the students are able to do meaningful work with their hands and create objects of beauty with a teacher who is a skilled craftsman. The students, in my experience, begin to learn actually to think with their hands. One acquires a capacity of the hands—a kind of physical intelligence—so that when one touches a material, the material will respond in an esthetic direction.

A Waldorf school in Germany (the Hibernia School) had a bakery on campus which was student-run. It gave students a place to go to recreate and to socialize, and all the goods of the bakery were sold, and the profits used to support the school, the class trip, and to offer small salaries. The students learned bookkeeping, ordering, how to deal with excess products, and so on. It was a tremendously successful social initiative. Not only was it a practical undertaking, but one of those students went on to become a baker as a profession and was very happy in his lifework.

High school teachers have to sit together and analyze their resources and ask what the abilities are within their own faculty. Next, they have to look out into the community to see what craft activities exist and might be associated with the school. If possible, involve these craftspeople, but involve them from a plan that has its basis in the anthroposophical Waldorf curriculum. The faculty has to make the decision of how the practical arts program, the manual arts, and the handwork program can flourish in their particular high school.

The important thing is to have people who are really capable in what they're doing and have an empathy for teenagers and for all the difficulties they go through.

A craftsperson can come in from the outside as long as he or she is given a clear picture of what is to happen. Experienced teachers have to be present at the beginning of the classes to make sure the social situation and the discipline are held in check. The Waldorf school in Ann Arbor brings the students to the studio of a local blacksmith, and they actually have the class in his functioning blacksmithing shop. This seems to be going very successfully. But the whole plan of the project was designed by the blacksmith together with the rest of the faculty. The responsibility was not assigned just to the blacksmith. The planning of the experience became as important as the teaching.

There are two schools of thought on whether crafts should be tracked or offered as an elective. Many of our Waldorf high schools require both boys and girls to experience similar handwork and practical arts or crafts projects in grades nine, ten, and eleven. Another school of thought creates a package of crafts electives and allows the students to choose which ones they will take. The individual advisors keep the students moving in the ninth and tenth grades so that they really experience all of the different crafts and handwork and do not begin to specialize until they become older, in the eleventh or twelfth grade. It is quite satisfying for an eleventh or twelfth grader to be able to carry something to greater depth, not to the point that that's the only thing that he or she is doing, but so that the student can achieve a certain perfection and quality of skill because of extra time spent.

There have been students who have gone into pottery and have chosen to become potters for life. The same is true with carpentry; there have been house builders who have become inspired through their high school curriculum. At this age the students can recognize aspects of their destiny.

The ninth-grade projects should consist of genuine work and a deepening understanding of the world. Students should be helped to feel that the world is theirs and that their feet are solidly placed upon its surface. Everything that man himself has created through the observation of nature and the recognition of its laws should be penetrated with comprehension. Rudolf Steiner wanted the immediate experience of life to be brought into the Waldorf school. He considered this so important that he recommended that the tenth grade specifically have several "Practical life Studies" (Lebenskunde) which, among other things, were to include mechanics, spinning, textile weaving, metal working, basketry, soap making, and surveying. This work began in the sixth grade when the children experienced practical work in manual arts and gardening.

Certain handwork and practical arts courses are developmentally important enough that all students in a Waldorf high school should participate in them. Those courses are: black and white construction in the ninth grade, clay modeling in the ninth and tenth grades, simple weaving with box loom and Inca loom in the tenth, bookbinding in the eleventh grade, and stone carving in the twelfth grade. Other subjects, such as weaving with the treadle looms, pottery, fabric making, papermaking and marbleizing, advanced sewing, more advanced blacksmithing, and copper chasing can be offered as electives.

In the high school, teachers must develop the curriculum so that the practical and studio arts are complementary to the main lesson. For example, the Faust main lesson in the twelfth grade, where students investigate the nature of the human soul, can be paired with stone carving, where students are challenged to create a sculpture of a human head. Another good match is bookbinding during either the Shakespeare block or Renaissance history.

Each craft project has its own procedure. First, the student must think or imagine the task; then she or he must prepare, research, and experiment. This is followed by a very important incubation period when the idea is allowed to rest, so that new directions may emerge. Then, the task is begun, completed, and reflected upon. Lastly, modifications are made. These activities exercise and integrate the thinking, the feeling, and the will life.

In the classroom we recognize three groups of students. There are those who make things happen. Then there are those who watch things happen, and finally, there are those who wonder what happened! Those students who are strengthened in their will activity are usually the ones who make things happen. They are confident in themselves and are not overly concerned about making a mistake. We must teach our students how to adapt the mistakes which they make, rather than start over again. The students must not be overly concerned with making mistakes, because fear of mistakes will cripple their progress. The only way to avoid mistakes is to avoid action. This is not something we want to encourage. What we want is courage and confidence, and this has been observed in those students who have mastered practical activities.

At puberty the adolescents are turned in on an inner world full of riddles which are difficult to understand. They hold something back from their outer expression, so that they can digest and absorb that which is moving them from this new inner space. During this time they begin to sense their own personal destiny. It is the concentration involved in true work, such as we find in the crafts and practical arts, which helps to bring about the proper relationship between that "inner" and "outer" space. This, seen from a social-human point of view, is now one of the main tasks in the high school.

Descriptions of craft activities follow:

Pottery

The first activity for the students in the pottery studio is to mix a variety of different clays. The bags of colored ground clay must be sifted and then proportionally mixed before students are ready to make pots by hand. They dig their fists into the moist clay and take up a snowball-sized piece. With their thumb they penetrate into the center, and with their forefinger they pinch and move around the pot until its sides are proportional. They allow it to dry for a day or two, glaze it, and fire it in the raku tradition in a metal bucket filled with sawdust. The sawdust is lit, and it smolders for a day or more before the vessel is lifted out.

Hand built 16-inch-high vase fired in raku tradition.

They continue to work with their hands, becoming more and more adept and more and more alive in their sense of touch. A final project might be the making by hand of two identical flower pots. They have to be congruent in every respect—this is no small task. When the teacher is satisfied, the pots are glazed, fired, and the student has graduated to the heel where cups, bowls, pitchers, plates, and the like, are thrown.

Here a mechanical device aids the hands, and the clay miraculously can rise and widen with an intended touch. Vessels can be replicated, and uniformity can be achieved.

The glazes and kiln-firing unite the potter with the chemist. Earth salts bring about fascinating colors, and the kiln fires the once supple clay into rigidity. Now we have a durable utensil.

Hand built coil pot fired in a gas kiln.

Two items thrown on a potters wheel.

Clay Sculpture

The first task for ninth graders is to take a piece of clay about the size of a grapefruit. Holding the clay near their sternum and the elbows of each arm pointed outward, the students use their hands to shape the clay into a perfect sphere. This position is important, because they should be using their entire upper body, shoulders and upper arms as well as their hands.

After the initial sphere is created, the elbows are bent, and now they experience the palm of the hand, the thumb, and the fingers as they press and shape the clay to spherical perfection. The final shape is consummated with gentle strokes of the finger.

When shaped as accurately as possible, the sphere is bisected with a cutting wire and the two pieces placed next to each other on a table so that they look like the number "8" with the convex portions upward. These two hemispheres are now worked together so that one becomes concave while the other remains convex. The form should be harmonious and peaceful, and the result should be a doubly bent "yin-yang"-shaped surface, with each side the inverted mirror image of the other. The project has moist towels placed over it, and it is covered with plastic so it will not dry out.

In the next class the first project is revisited, and a new task is put before the students. They must now transform this convex/concave shape into a sleeping or embryonic animal of their choice.

The next exercise is one dealing with metamorphosis: the students take their sleeping animal, and once again create a sphere. They place the completed sphere on a table and press down into it, so that they create an ellipse the actual size of a baby's head. From this shape they create the full physiognomy of a one-year-old. Wonderful discussions can evolve about the fullness of the baby's cheeks, the mere semblance of a chin, the tall forehead and peaked head, and the overall feeling of moistness and fullness. The students are allowed to use sculpting sticks and wires, as they bring their sculpture to perfection.

In the next class, they take the baby physiognomy and transform it into an adolescent. The features become more distinct and individual. When completed, the teenager is metamorphosed into a forty-year-old and then finally into a person of old age, past seventy. Now the sculpture has features that are exaggerated. The skin has become wrinkled, the nose more prominent, the forehead more open like the baby's. In contrast to the baby, though, one notices the absence of the fluid element. Now we see bone and tight skin.

The final exercise in this series is to transform the old person into a gargoyle. Many have been itching to do this all along, and it is great fun. One can cup the hands on either side of the head and twist it inward. The nose will expand, the eyes will distort, and "another world" form will emerge.

A variation on this exercise is to take any of the older physiognomies and transform the face from happiness to sadness, or vice versa.

The students are encouraged to study and observe each other's faces. This is a wonderful social exercise.

In the tenth grade one can start with a large piece of clay and ask the students to create a full-form head of a lion, an eagle, or a bull. Be sure that the clay is substantial enough so that the sculpting is not just finger-work.

For the next exercise I show the students the following slides of Ernst Barlach's wood carvings: *"der Sparzlergänger," "Zwei Figuren vom Fries der Lauschenden," "der Gläubige, die Begnadete," "Frierende Alte,"* and *"der Wanderer."* These carvings show amazing facial expressions.

The students are asked to create an eight-inch-high human being expressing either an inner or an outer gesture.

Inner gesture	*Outer gesture*
thinking joy despair, etc.	pulling or pushing something carrying a weight lifting something heavy, etc.

First, they build a pillar, shape the head from the top, and then move into the gesture.

Another exercise consists of having the students roll clay donuts. They take a piece of clay and roll it into a sausage. They form these into a coil pot the size of a human head. Then they work with two hands: the outside one holds the action of the hand working on the inside from pushing too far, and from the inside they create a human head. The knuckle of the inside hand pushes out the nose while the other hand holds it back, and so forth. The back can be left open.

A variation of this is to add plaster to make a mold and then mold a positive plaster cast.

If you are fortunate enough to have the clay sculpting continue into the eleventh and twelfth grades, you can add armatures and do full-scale models.

Basketry

Baskets can be made from willow, reeds, grasses, bark, and strips of wood. The material must be soaked in water to be made supple. In the case of wooden baskets the elm logs are soaked for a year and then, in the spring, hammered with two-pound broadfaced hammers until the inner structure of the wood loosens, and 3/4 to 1-inch-wide strips can be peeled off with a knife. These strips need to be kept moist until the basket is finished. The shape of the basket should suit the purpose, and each material has a different technique which is easily learned.

Baskets made with ash strips.

After a year soaking in the pond, the logs are brought to shore on a warm spring day.

In the making of a wood-strip basket one makes a flat weave the size of the bottom of the basket. A pine board the size of the bottom is placed over the weave and the moist and supple strips are bent up to make the sides. The weave is continued and the board is removed. This rectangular shape is strong, prohibits distortion, and is quite rigid when completed. Basket weaving is similar to textile weaving. The repetitious, geometric activity

Pounding the soaked logs with heavy hammers loosens the fibers which can then be pealed back with knives.

is very soothing to the soul, the end-product is both useful and aesthetically pleasing.

Macramé

Mythology is full of stories connecting weaving and knot tying with wisdom. Two examples are the puzzle of the Gordian knot, which Oedipus solved, and Theseus' winding out the thread from the Labyrinth on Crete, through its mysterious thousand paths. Theseus defeated the Minotaur by means of string and cleverness. Athena, who was born out of the head of Zeus and ruled over the world of thoughts, was called the inspirer of all arts and crafts. It is crafts that teach students to meet and overcome problems. They become engaged in an activity which, on the one hand, focuses them and, on the other hand, can lead them through the eye of the needle by which process they become transformed.

Macramé is an important craft in the curriculum. We first must identify a starting point for the shaping of the intertwined knots. This time we begin with a spiral movement and come to rest in crossing. This activity requires wakefulness. It is complicated to arrange the knots out of which the shape of the piece of work is to come. Different knots, such as the clove hitch used by many American Indian tribes, are learned and are used depending upon the pattern.

Equipment

Each project will present its own unique set of challenges, but there is a set of factors that all macramé projects have in common.

One should always have sufficient light to work with, and preferably some light source behind, which shines on the work itself. One also needs plenty of room, as there will be many lengths of string to work with. The space should be clean, since the medium will pick up whatever it comes in contact with: lint, hair, dirt, dust balls, and so forth, which will thus be incorporated into the finished piece.

Anything which can serve as a line can be used in macramé: yarn, string, twine, floss, jute, macramé yarn, and the like. However, some mediums are better than others, as, for example, jute which is strong and substantial to work with, although it can be hard on the hands.

Most macramé pieces are attached to something—rings, dowels, driftwood, belt buckles, formed wire, or the like. These objects are also utilized in the patterns themselves. Fondue skewers make fine dowels for small pieces. Old lamp shade rings, if they are not welded together, are excellent sources for rings. And never forget the vast reservoir of materials available at yard sales. All the basic tools needed for macramé are readily available at craft shops or department stores.

Except for three-dimensional and free-formed pieces, all macramé has to be pinned down. Therefore, you will need T-pins (wig or hat pins), and something to pin the piece to. A cardboard corrugated box is by far the best—it holds the pins, and, thus, the piece, down better than Styrofoam, cork, or polyurethane. It also does not come apart when the pins are repeatedly stuck in and pulled out.

A clean toothbrush is a good tool to remove lint and dust from a project. Also, a good sharp pair of scissors is a must. A wise investment is plastic embroidery floss holders. In very large pieces, in which the lines are very long, it is vital to bundle the medium into small packages. This prevents them from tangling, and makes them easier to work with. Small, short pieces do not require this extra step (lines less than about 3 to 4 yards). A metal yard stick is of tremendous help in keeping the piece straight, even for the experienced craftsperson.

Tying on

Most macramé projects are started by tying the medium onto some stationary object, such as a dowel, a metal ring, or a preformed wire frame. The most common way utilized is with two half hitches, one right-handed and the other left-handed. The addition of the two half hitches creates the space necessary for square knots, clove hitches, or whatever knot you are creating to be tied on the next row.

Hang a dowel on each end. Cut the yarn to the desired length and double it over, forming a small loop at the mid-point. Slide the loop under the dowel with one hand, and grasp it with the other.

Fold it over the dowel and across the vertical lines of the remainder of the yarn. With your thumb and first finger inside the loop, grasp the two interior vertical lines and pull them up and through the loop. Pull the resulting knot snug, but not tight.

It is now time to add the half hitch knots. Half hitch knots are not true knots, as they require another knot to complete them. They are actually one half of a clove hitch knot—thus, the name.

Now proceed to follow the design and knotting pattern for your project.

Spinning, Dyeing, Weaving

Spinning is the first task that meets the students when they enter the weaving studio. Each student is taught how to process and wash raw wool, how to prepare worsted and woolen yarns using wool combs and hand carders, as well as how to operate a drum carder and dress a distaff that holds their fiber while they spin. They are taught to spin on a variety of spindles, such as the high whorl, low whorl, Turkish, hand spindle, Navajo, and Tahkli spindle, to make a two- and three-ply yarn. They learn about different types of wools and their uses for different styles of yarn. After they have spun a sufficient amount of single yarns, the students learn how to ply them together to make suitable yarns for knitting or weaving.

Inspired during the main lesson block on Faust, a student free-wove this portrait.

Some students learn how to spin some of the more exotic fibers, such as mohair, silks of all kinds, camel, llama and alpaca, and ramie.

Next the students learn how to dye wool, cotton, and linen threads using only simple household chemicals and the colors extracted from plant barks, berries, flowers, leaves, and insects. They explore indigo for blues; cochineal and brazilwood for reds and purples; madder root for orange-reds; osage orange and fustic for yellows, golds, and greens; cutch and walnut crystals for browns; logwood for lavenders and black; safflower for yellows and reds. The students also learn over-dyeing to show how unrelated colors can be made to work together introducing a new color family.

Finally, they are ready to weave on a loom. The students learn to read a threading draft and explain all the different parts of a draft—the threading, the tie-up, and treadling. They learn how to determine the treadling by analyzing the threading and then how to decipher the tie-up for four harnesses and multi-harnesses, such as the Harrisville Design floor looms and the Cranbrook looms. They learn about the old weavers' customs for treadling Star fashion, Rose fashion, and on opposites. Each student is then shown how to do a drawdown on graph paper, so they can see how their patterns will look when woven.

Some students experience the Navajo loom. Navajo weaving is special. The Navajo loom is peaceful, meditative, quiet. One learns to enjoy the process and not be anxious about a finished product. The Navajo have a unique way of dressing their loom so the unfinished weaving is very portable, and the finished weaving has no fringe and is reversible. This tapestry technique creates a firm structure suitable for rugs, vests, carrying bags, pillow covers, saddle blankets, as well as wall hangings.

There has been a renewal of weaving rag rugs in the last several years. What was once considered a frugal way of recycling old clothing into rugs has become an art form. Students weave samples of different patterns and weave structures in a round robin format. Samples are woven to useful place mat size. Some of the weave structures learned, besides plain weave variations, include warpface, weftface, twill, rep, and log cabin.

Fabrics

The woven material is transformed into clothing in the fabrics class, where students learn to make patterns, measure, cut, and sew clothing.

First, they make a sketch of an article of clothing and then create a pattern which must be pinned onto the piece of fabric. Spatial imagination is required for pattern-making. and the refinement of individuality occurs in creating unique and appropriate clothing for oneself as a teenager. Geometry and measurements are crucial and must be executed accurately. Otherwise, the fabric will not properly piece together, and, in the end, after hours of labor, may not fit. The whole project will succeed only if everything has been contemplated, drawn, and measured accurately. Only after the process has been carefully thought through can the action begin. Now the material is cut into pieces and then put back together in correct order with the help of a sewing machine. The students learn that careful planning combined with precise execution result in an article of clothing they can wear with pride.

Batik

by Ruth Pittman

A studio offering in batik can provide high school students with a challenging, creative, and rewarding experience. Originally an ancient Indonesian textile art, batik is now recognized in the United States and elsewhere as a major contemporary fiber art.

The distinguishing features of batik, which in Indonesian means "drawing in wax," are the unique qualities of line from the traditional *tjanting*, or wax pen, and the beautiful harmonious sequences of colors provided by the transparent dyes. The students are encouraged to allow the materials to speak out of their own qualities. For example, the flowing line of wax from the *tjanting* tool may suggest rhythms in nature: rising-falling, angular-spiraling, swelling-diminishing. Practicing the difficult skill of drawing with the wax, of slowly achieving one's vision, develops patience and a willingness to work, to do the best with what one has, to go on and try again. The batiking process encourages students' artistic abilities to grow in important ways, including creating form, envisioning the whole, and achieving harmony and unity in their work.

With practice, students find the tjanting to be an exciting and versatile tool through which they may discover—or rediscover—a new possibility of expression. They may discover within themselves unrealized artistic faculties, and feelings of ineptness may give way to growing confidence in their own creative abilities. The unusual materials and process of batik call on students to be open to the new and unexpected—happy surprises—as well as accidents, such as sudden dripping of the wax. Having to think and then rethink the steps throughout the process allows for new ideas to develop, but more importantly, gives rise to a growing awareness of the nature of these materials. The development of respect and understanding for the craft opens the way for students to approach it with both modesty and joy in creating out of themselves, freely, freshly.

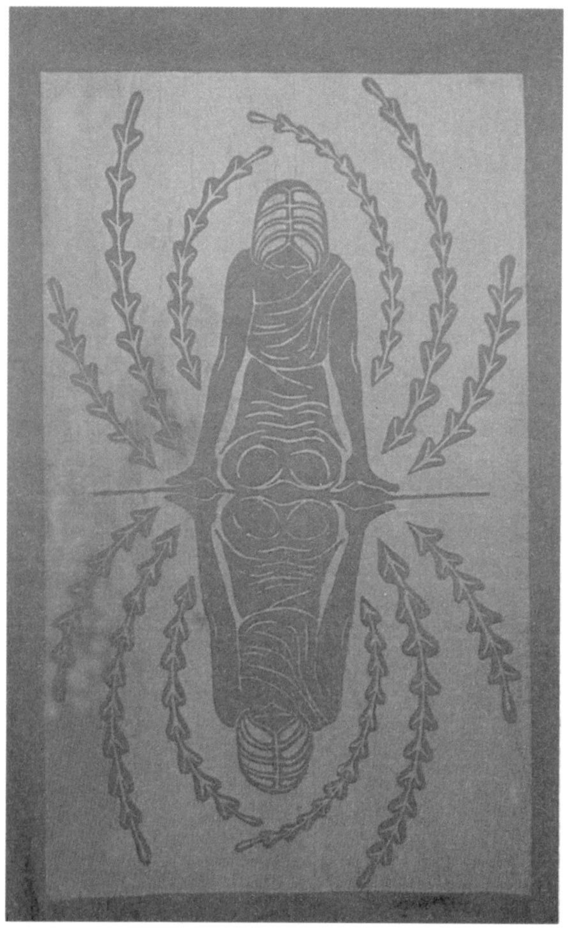

Batik is based on the principle of resist, which is a means of preventing dye from penetrating wax lines or areas of fabric. The wax repels the dye. The process depends upon successive applications of melted wax and immersions of the fabric in dye baths, so that the colors move in a progression from light to dark, bright to dull, warm to cool. The last step involves ironing out the wax between layers of newsprint or paper towels, revealing the complete image.

The waxing and dyeing process involves a variety of decisions to be made with each step. There is always the need to attend to the aesthetic aspect: color relationships, form, rhythm, pattern, space, to wax or not to wax. Thus, the interest of students is quite easily sustained throughout. They become devoted to their work and bring warmth to it.

The unpredictability of the waxing and dyeing process can be challenging as well as frustrating, despite well-developed skills: wax may spill, or unexpected colors appear. This uncertainty invites students to care about their work, to hope as well as be anxious about the outcome—all part of this creative experience. Unpredictability is something many students seem to relish. They can bring a stunning life-giving spontaneity as well as originality to their projects when a bit of risk is combined and controlled by their new expertise.

Most students plan more complex projects on paper first to help them envision the end result. Over-planning though can deaden inspiration, and yet insufficient planning can create chaos. Eventually, students find their own balance in preserving the vitality of their work.

Unlike traditional drawing and painting, mistakes can be difficult, if not impossible to remove, but with some creative, positive thinking, most mistakes can be turned into "lucky accidents," enhancing the project and even leading to new ideas in thinking through artistic and technical elements. Also, in batik there is the magic inherent in the technique itself contributing to the beauty of the work—especially in helping to unify the various parts.

In the studio the batik table serves as a center for creative, communal activity. Students share the wax, the tools, the space, and studio responsibilities. Warm, mutual support and respect prevail.

Beginning students are given ample time to freely explore waxing with the tjanting tool. Samples may be created to practice unifying design elements in pattern making and in layering of colors. Further projects may then be planned for specific uses: scarves, pillow covers, tote bags, shirts, skirts, wall hangings, and more painterly expressive images, which may be stretched on canvas stretchers and framed if desired.

All aspects of batik help to make for a well-appreciated craft. And besides, as students often say, it's fun!

Woodworking

by David Mitchell

Our first concern is the layout of the high school joinery shop. The space must be safe, with adequate light, ventilation, and storage.

The first priority is to draw the space to scale on a piece of graph paper and imagine the work flow from raw wood through to the finishing stages of a project. Place the storage area for new wood convenient to the outside. Now, place those tools necessary for stock preparation in an adjacent open space (like the jointer, table saw, and thickness planer).

Each tool has its own space requirements. This isn't just the visible "footprint" of the tool. But more importantly, it is the extra space needed so that the material that feeds in (or out) of one tool does not intrude on another one. Because of the clearance required in front, back, and at the sides when cutting large workpieces, the table saw usually claims more than its fair share of space, so this is the first item to position.

Once the stock is made flat, straight, and square, the next step is to use the jointer to shape the pieces. To make this go smoothly, position the drill press, router table, and band saw near the workbenches. By locating the workbenches out in the open, there is access on all sides, which makes it easy to assemble projects and move about.

The corners of a shop often get filled with clutter. I like to place the drill press in the corner and take advantage of what could become wasted space. Once you have determined the locations of your major tools, have an electrician place the appropriate plugs so that electrical wires will not be tripping people.

Try to place all the tools for specific functions in the same area. All the saws can hang in one area, the planes, spokeshaves and scrapers in another, and so on. Help the students develop the habit of putting everything back in the proper place.

Try to take advantage of doors and windows. Positioning a band saw or table saw near a door will assist you on those extra-long pieces that have to be cut. The shop should inspire students to work by the organized and professional atmosphere that greets them. The space for "carving" can be far less complicated.

As mentioned earlier, woodworking divides into two directions in the high school. One direction pursues the more artistic side of carving: wood sculpture, gouged bowls, turned bowls and vases made on the wood lathe, and the like. The other direction involves furniture making, joinery, and building construction. Both encourage aesthetic sensitivity, but the first is more delicate, whereas the second is more willful.

Both of these directions can, and should, lead the student toward developing real skills and expertise. In cabinetry they should be taught how to safely use the basic power tools, the table saw, the drill press, the planer, the jointer, and the power sander. They should be familiar with various joinery techniques, such as making spline joints, dowel joints, biscuit joints, mortise and tenon joints, as well as the dovetail.

Examples of Cabinetry Projects

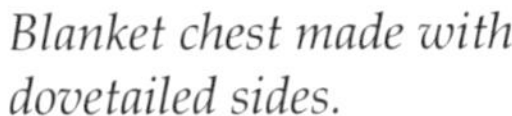
Blanket chest made with dovetailed sides.

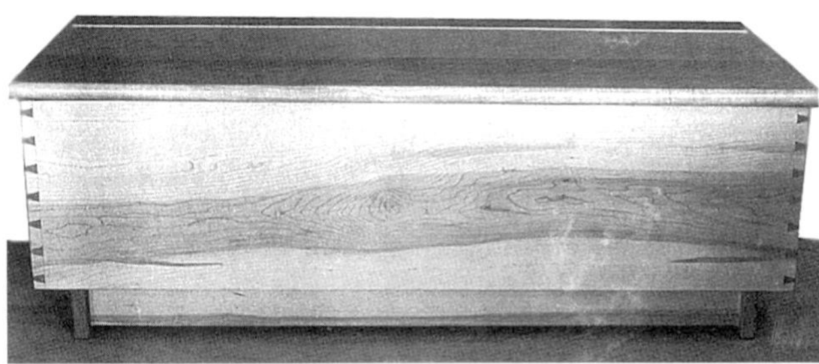

Table made with mortise and tenon joints.

Trestle table.
– Photo by Ed Edelstein

Stool made with a drawknife and a bit and brace.
–Photo by Ed Edelstein

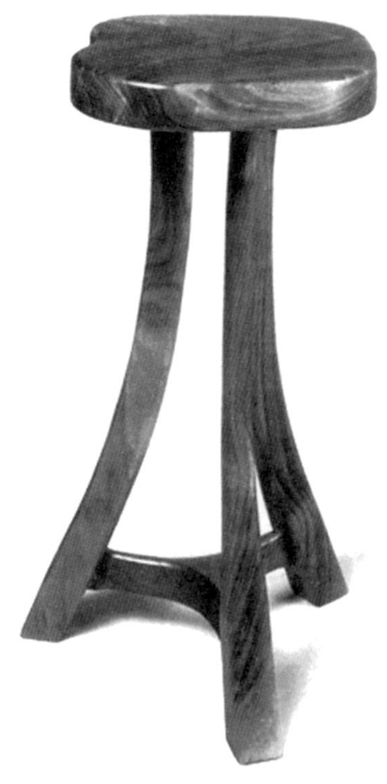

Advanced stool made from mahogany.

Student showing a smile of accomplishment upon completion of her guitar.
–Photo by Ed Edelstein

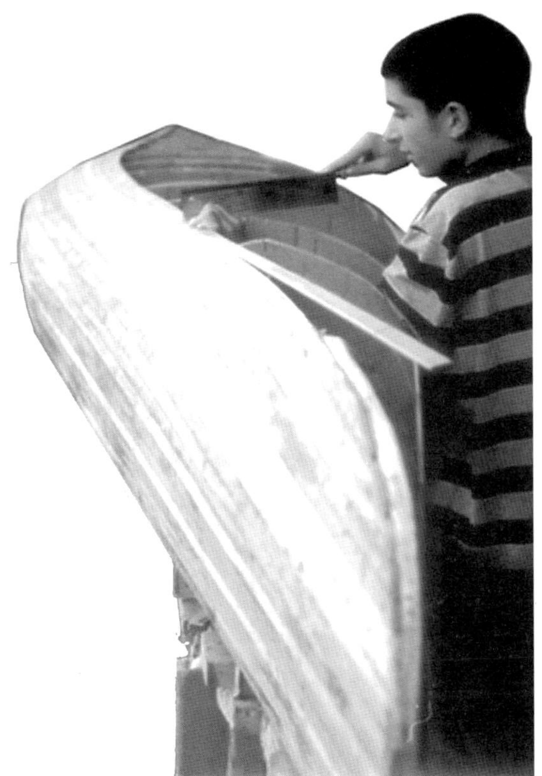

The Toronto Waldorf School builds kayaks and canoes.

–Photo by Ed Edelstein

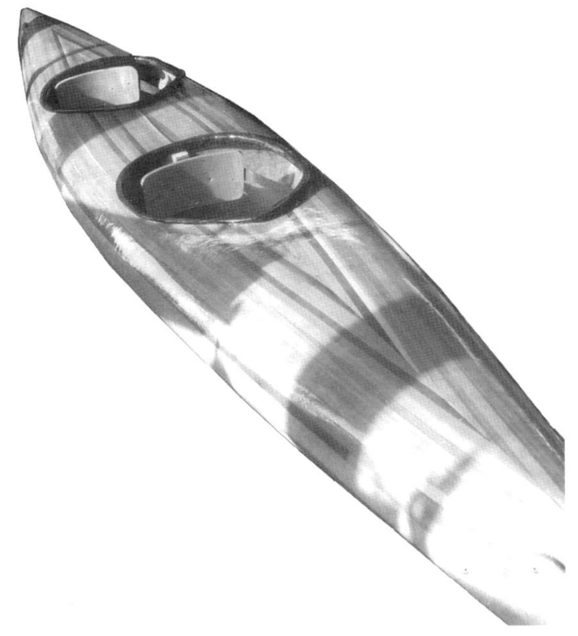

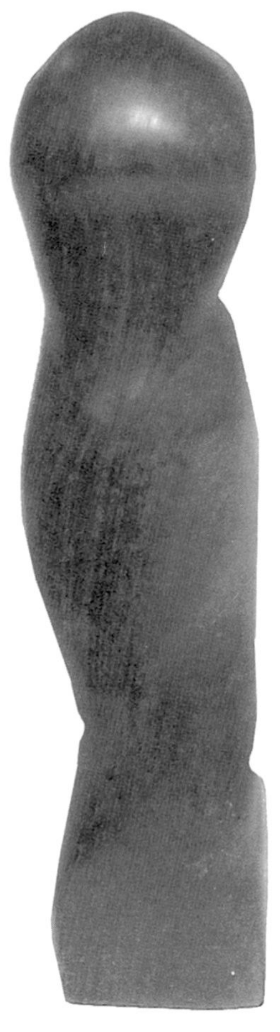

Sculpture in teak using only a rasp and scrapers.

Exercise in sugarpine involving harmonious movement.

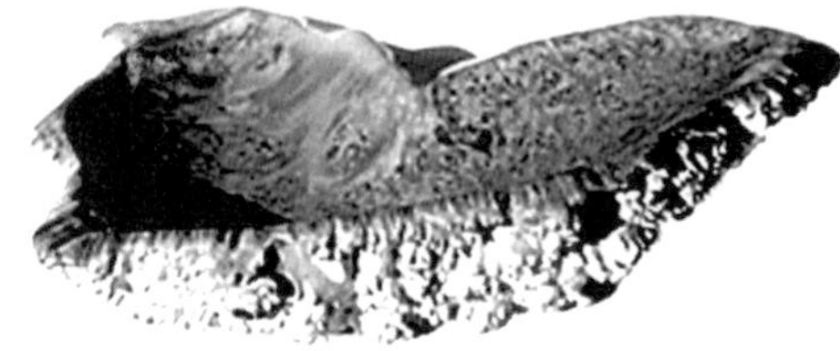

Bowl carved from a maple burl.

Bowl carved from elm.

Bowl and candleholder carved from linden.

A carved clockface.
– Photo by Ed Edelstein

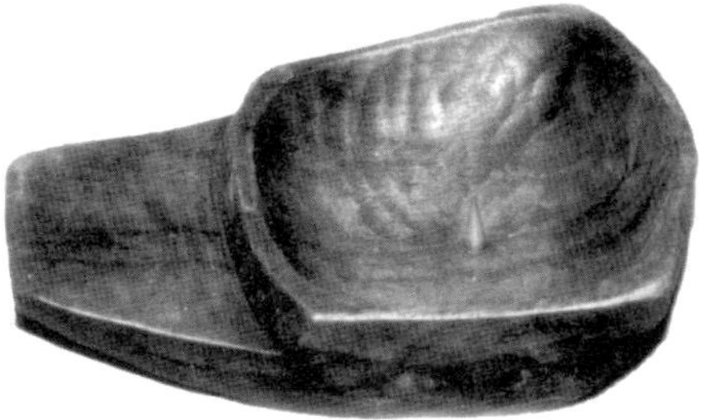

Walnut candleholder with a sharpened brass screw in the center to hold the candle.

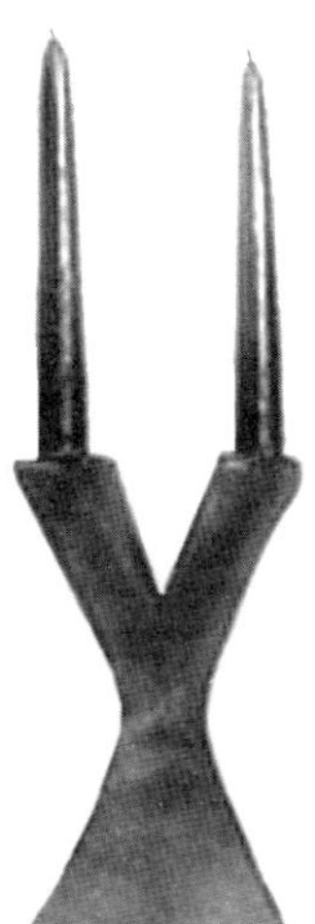

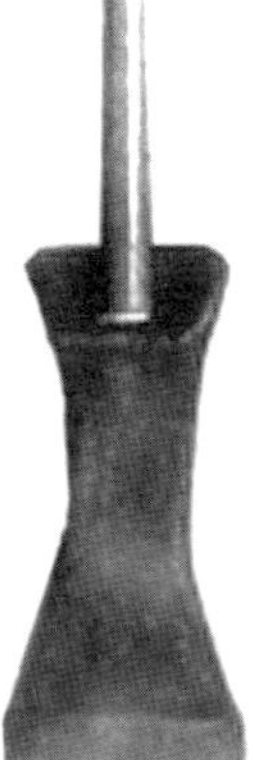

Exercise in metamorphosis involving three candleholders.

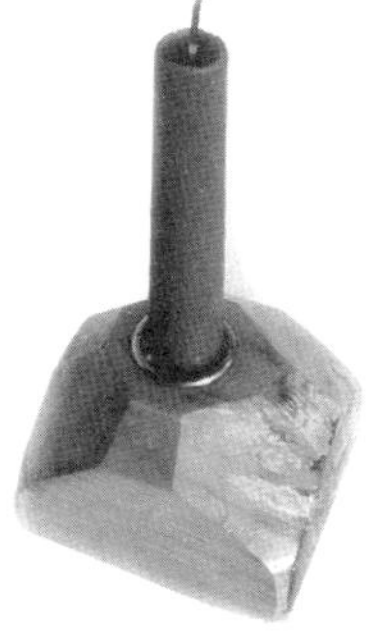

Simple geometric maple candleholder.

Sculpture of a sitting woman in walnut.

Artistic projects in wood for main lesson

In the main lesson a teacher can assign the students the possibility of doing a course-related artistic project. This can be a stained glass window during the history block on the Middle Ages, the carving of an animal for zoology, the modeling of the baby in the womb for embryology. The possibilities are limitless.

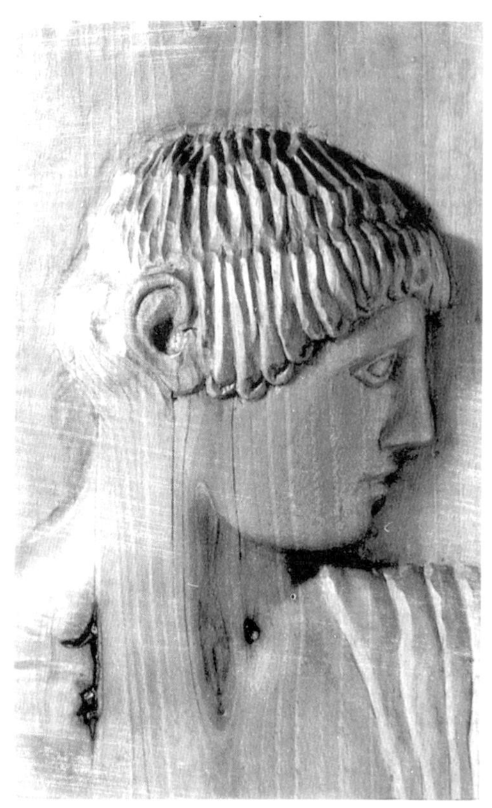

Apollo, carved out of olive wood for ancient history.

A hedgehog carved for zoology.

A raptor in flight carved for zoology.

WOOD DESCRIPTION CHART

HARDWOODS

Species	Comparative Weights	Color	Ease of Working	Relative Density	General Strength	Resistance to Decay	Wood finishing	Cost
Ash, Brown	Medium	Light Brown	Medium	Hard	Medium	Low	Medium	Medium/high
Ash, Tough White	Heavy	Off-White	Hard	Hard	Good	Low	Medium	Medium
Ash, Soft White	Medium	Off-White	Medium	Medium	Low	Low	Medium	Medium/Low
Avodire	Medium	Golden Blond	Medium	Medium	Low	Low	Medium	High
Balsawood	Light	Cream White	Easy	Soft	Low	Low	Poor	Medium
Basswood	Light	Cream White	Easy	Soft	Low	Low	Medium	Medium
Beech	Heavy	Light Brown	Hard	Hard	Good	Low	Easy	Medium
Birch	Heavy	Light Brown	Hard	Hard	Good	Low	Easy	High
Butternut	Light	Light Brown	Easy	Soft	Low	Medium	Medium	Medium
Cherry, Black	Medium	Medium Reddish Brown	Poor	Hard	Good	Medium	Easy	High
Chestnut	Light	Light Brown	Medium	Medium	Medium	High	Poor	Medium
Cottonwood	Light	Greyish White	Medium	Soft	Low	Low	Poor	Low
Elm, Soft Grey	Medium	Cream Tan	Hard	Medium	Medium	Medium	Medium	Medium/Low
Gum, Red	Medium	Reddish Brown	Medium	Medium	Medium	Medium	Medium	Medium/High
Hickory, True	Heavy	Reddish Tan	Hard	Hard	Good	Low	Medium	Low
Holly	Medium	White to Grey	Medium	Hard	Medium	Low	Easy	Medium
Korina	Medium	Pale Golden	Medium	Medium	Medium	Low	Medium	High
Magnolia	Medium	Yellowish Brown	Medium	Medium	Medium	Low	Easy	Medium
Mahogany, Honduras	Medium	Golden Brown	Easy	Medium	Medium	High	Medium	High
Mahogany, Philippine	Medium	Medium Red	Good	Medium	Medium	High	Medium	Medium/High
Maple, Hard	Heavy	Reddish Cream	Hard	Hard	Good	Low	Easy	Medium/High
Maple, Soft	Medium	Reddish Brown	Hard	Hard	Good	Low	Easy	Medium/Low
Oak, Red (Average)	Heavy	Flesh Brown	Hard	Hard	Good	Low	Medium	Medium
Oak, White (Average)	Heavy	Greyish Brown	Hard	Hard	Good	High	Medium	Medium/High
Poplar, Yellow	Medium	Light to Dark Yellow	Good	Soft	Low	Low	Easy	Medium
Prima Vera	Medium	Straw Tan	Medium	Medium	Medium	Medium	Medium	High
Sycamore	Medium	Flesh Brown	Hard	Medium	Medium	Low	Easy	Medium/Low
Walnut, Black	Heavy	Dark Brown	Medium	Hard	Good	High	Medium	High
Willow, Black	Light	Medium Brown	Easy	Soft	Low	Low	Medium	Medium/Low

SOFTWOODS

Species	Comparative Weights	Color	Ease of Working	Relative Density	General Strength	Resistance to Decay	Wood finishing	Cost
Cedar, Tennessee Red	Medium	Red	Poor	Medium	Medium	High	Easy	Medium
Cypress	Medium	Yellow to Reddish Brown	Good	Soft	Medium	High	Poor	Medium/High
Fir, Douglas	Medium	Orange-Brown	Medium	Soft	Medium	Medium	Poor	Medium
Fir, White	Light	Nearly White	Medium	Soft	Low	Low	Poor	Low
Pine, Yellow Longleaf	Medium	Orange to Reddish Brown	Hard	Medium	Good	Medium	Medium	Medium
Pine, Northern White (Pinus Strobus)		Light Cream to Reddish Brown	Easy	Soft	Low	Medium	Medium	Medium/High
Pine, Ponderosa	Light	Orange to Reddish Brown	Easy	Soft	Low	Low	Medium	Medium
Pine, Sugar	Light	Creamy Brown	Easy	Soft	Low	Medium	Poor	Medium/High
Redwood	Light	Deep Reddish Brown	Easy	Soft	Medium	High	Poor	Medium
Spruce (Average)	Light	Nearly White	Medium	Soft	Low	Low	Medium	Medium

Steps for making a dovetail joint:

The optimum slope of a dovetail joint depends upon the type of wood you are using. Softwoods should have a slope ratio of 1 in 6, while hardwoods should have a 1 in 8 angle: that is one "unit" in from the side for every 8 units along the length of the wood. It is worth making a dovetail template to each of these proportions if you intend to make a number of dovetail joints, or, like me, you can purchase one made out of indestructible brass from a woodworking store, like Woodcraft Supply in Woburn, Massachusetts. Not only will it speed the process up somewhat, but it will also ensure a uniformity between the joints.

1. Set the marker gauge to the thickness of the "male" tail-pin wood, and mark this thickness all around the "female" receptor piece. Then set the gauge to the thickness of the "female" piece, and mark all around the "male" tail-pin piece.

2. On the end of the "male" tail-pin piece, draw a line across the end that is half the thickness of the "female" wood. For example, if the "female" piece is 1" thick, this line will be drawn 1/2" in from the end of the "male" tail-pin piece. Repeat this for the other end of the "male" tail- pin piece as well, so that you have a matching line.

3. Measure the distance between these two lines and subtract 1/4" for each pin, less one. For example, if you plan to have six pins, and the distance between the two end lines is 7 1/4", subtract FIVE (i.e., six, less one) 1/4" gaps. The result is 6". Then, divide this number by the number of pins that you want (in this case six) to determine the size of each tail (in this case 1"). So, what you now have is six pins, each 1" wide, with a gap of 1/4" in between each one.

4. Once these end lines have all been draw out, mark out the tail slopes (at either a 1 in 8 or 1 in 6 ratio, depending on whether you use hard wood or soft wood).

5. Use a sharp backsaw and saw out the "male" tail-pins. To do this, clamp the wood at an angle so that the saw cut is vertical. This makes cutting the desired angle far easier. Always cut just to the inside of your marks so that the joint will fit tightly.

6. Once the "male" tail-pins have been cut out, clamp the "female" piece vertically in a vice. Then, using the

"male" tail-pin piece as a template, mark out the shape of the female pins on the end of the "female" piece with a very sharp pencil or a steel scribe. Once this is done (and it must be very accurate), draw these lines down to the thickness line done in step 1.

7. Cut out the "female" pin holes, being very careful to cut inside the line.

8. Once the pins have been cut carefully test them to see if they fit. If they are too tight use a flat bastard file gently on the "male" pins until they do. Check for fit frequently. The joint should be very stiff.

9. When it fits snugly you can choose to lock them together with a 1/4" dowel set snugly in a drilled hole from the top, or you can glue them.

Pattern Transferring

To transfer a complicated pattern to a piece of wood you can use a simple trick. Take a photocopy of the pattern and an ordinary household iron. With the photocopy taped face down on the piece of wood, slowly move a clothes iron (set on high) back and forth. The heat from the iron reactivates the toner on the photocopy and transfers the image to the wood.

Stained Glass

While the students are studying the Middle Ages, a course in stained class is appropriate.

The Golden Age of Gothic Architecture began in the 1100s when Abbe Sugar added to his Abbey Church of St. Denis, near Paris, "the most radiant windows" to "illuminate men's minds so that they may travel through their light to an apprehension of God's light."

Colored glass then became used in all medieval churches because of their spiritual quality, sensual appeal, and a belief that certain illnesses could be healed through the combination of meditative prayer and specific colors. The Bible makes many references to color. In Genesis, the colorful rainbow is referred to as God's Covenant with man after the Flood. The art of stained glass not only provided beauty and comfort, but was instructional for the illiterate people of the times, because of the stories conveyed through their designs.

Today the oldest, complete, existing stained glass windows still in their original site are in the Augsburg Cathedral in Germany. These are the famous "Prophets" windows, and they were made in the eleventh century.

The basic concept begins with the creating of a full-size "cartoon" showing the design; then comes the shaping of the pieces of glass, wrapping the individual pieces of glass with strips of lead came (or copper foil), and the joining together of all the various pieces with solder.

Solder is the metal used to join lead or copper foil wrapped around the pieces of glass. A soft solder of tin/lead alloy melts easily. The numbers used to identify solder refer to the mixture of tin and lead, with the first number referring to the tin content. The two types most frequently used are 50/40 and 60/40. A 60/40 solder melts at a lower temperature than a 50/50.

The Tiffany Company perfected the copper foil technique, which allowed them to make lightweight glass items. The secret to working with copper foil is: accurate glass cutting, flat edges on the glass, tight crimping of the foil, and strong solder beads. A glass grinder is a necessity to make the glass have a smooth edge and fit accurately.

Bookbinding and Boxmaking

I refer to the eleventh grade bookbinding class as "Logical Thinking 101," because the student must proceed in a step-by-step manner, where each step requires precision and care, and linear thinking is exercised.

Rudolf Steiner said more about the necessity of bookbinding than about any other subject.

> *Out of self-knowledge I am able to modestly say, that I could not have spoken about certain things in spiritual science if I had not learned book binding at a certain age. The activity of bookbinding gives to our most intimate spirit-soul being something very special, particularly if it occurs at the right stage of human development. It is the same for all practical activities.*
>
> *I would consider it a sin against the being of man if, at the correct time of human development, subjects such as bookbinding, box-making and cardboard-work were not taken into the curriculum. These subjects belong to the making of a truly whole human being. Not the fact that one has produced this or that box or bound this or that book is important; what is essential is that one has gone through the process demanded in their execution—that one has experienced the feelings, the thought-processes in their practical doing.*

Tools needed include: benches, a lying-press, a plough, a millboard cutter, a cutting clamp, a nipping press, a sewing frame, a gluepot and brush, and several bricks wrapped in cloth (for weights).

The students first make a box with a lid out of cardboard, which has been bound in vellum, leather, marbleized paper, or a watercolor painting they have executed. Next, they make a small one-signature blank book with a hardboard cover.

After successfully completing these projects, they take on a book. The steps taken are:

Fold and collate the sections.
Press them flat overnight; make endpapers.
Mark and sew the signatures.
Attach special endpapers.
Glue the spine.
Cut the edges.
Round the back.
Clean off spine and put in press to dry.
Line spine with mull and paper.
Design and cut the hardboard cover to size.
Cut the stiffener for the case.
Make the case.
Paste down endpapers and press.
Sew the decorative header.
Apply decoration such as gold leaf stamping.

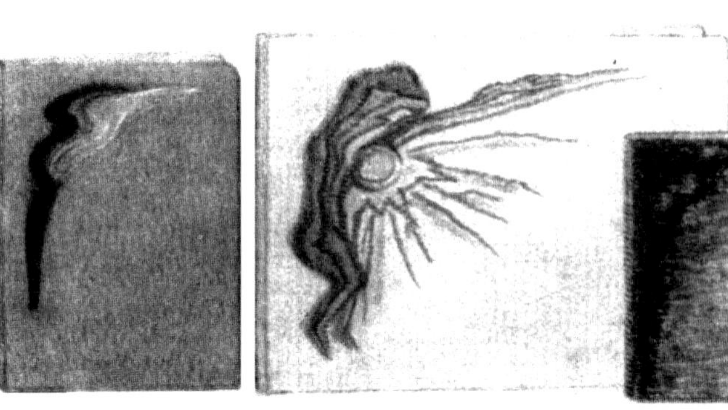

Papermaking

Rudolf Steiner wanted the manufacturing of paper taught in grade eleven. The oldest paper was found in China at the time of Emperor Wuti (141-86 B.C.). The bound collection of papers that we call a book was developed in the monasteries of the early Middle Ages and has always been rectangular, but its precursors had spiral forms, like the papyrus rolls of the Egyptians. The Greeks and Romans used bands of paper spirally wrapped around a staff, which were wrapped around a second staff with the other hand in counter-movement, while being read.

The papermaking process begins with shredded fibers of paper, cloth (one-inch squares of linen or cotton work best), or natural plant fiber, which are placed in a heavy duty blender, mixed with water, and blended into a pulp.

The pulp is poured into a vat, a container that holds the pulp and water solution, and more water is added. A two-part screen called a mould and deckle is scooped into the vat toward the papermaker, then pulled up through the water, allowing excess water to drain off through the screen. The mould and deckle is a separation device for dividing the pulp from the water. The bottom half is called the mould. It is a wooden frame with a fine screen stapled to it. The top portion, or deckle, is a wooden frame that fits over the outside edges of the mould.

The pulp forms a layer that bonds as it dries on the surface of the mould, and that's what we know as paper. The amount of pulp added to the vat will control the thickness of the sheet of paper. The newly formed sheet of paper is couched, or transferred from the surface of the mould to a piece of felt. Then, the paper is pressed and dried. The tools, dyes, and supplies needed to make handmade paper can be purchased, but with ingenuity one can scavenge the necessary materials.

Colored vegetable dyes may be used, but be sure to rinse the pulp thoroughly after dyeing, using a sieve. Try sprinkling colored threads, small petals and leaves, or glitter into the vats. Use your imagination. However, remember that these items should not be too large. They could be an obstacle when writing or even in keeping the outline of the paper crisp.

A simple way to marbleize paper is to secure a large vessel with low sides that will hold water. Fill it with water to within one inch of the top. Take some enamel oil paint and dribble paint onto the surface of the water. With a duck's feather, or other suitable long feather, stroke a pattern with the paint on the water's surface. When a pleasing pattern is created, lay a sheet of paper directly on top of the design and then pick it up, lifting one corner and peel the paper up. Allow the paper to dry overnight, cut to size, and you will have beautiful endpapers for the books you make in bookbinding.

Materials needed to make paper:

Fibers from paper or cloth
Felts (can use old blankets or old cotton sheets)
Tracing paper and pencil
Ruler / straight edge
X-acto knife with sharp blades
Typing paper
Heavy-duty blender
Dye pot(s)
Wooden spoon
Sieve
Sizing
Dry glue
Mould(s) and deckle(s)
Cutting surface (Formica/laminated masonite)
Scissors
Drying rack(s)
Staple gun
Colored pencil
Steam iron
Duct tape

Metalwork

Casting

To cast, we first make moulds of plaster in shallow plastic, flat-bottomed containers. Always add the plaster to the water, and when it reaches a creamy consistency, lift the container an inch above the table and carefully drop it several times. This should remove any trapped air bubbles.

When the plaster is hard, the students can take a pencil and draw the item to be cast on the surface. Next, micro chisels are used to carve out the plaster. Care must be taken to insure that the sides are perpendicular as well as uniform. All dust is blown away.

The next step is to heat the casting metal. I like to use a low melting ingot of pewter (which I purchase through Oster Pewter, Sims Street, Providence, Rhode Island 02900). We take a metal ladle, add the pewter, and heat it with a propane torch. Safety goggles must be worn throughout this entire process!

Now comes the pour. Carefully, we ladle the hot metal into the prepared carving in the plaster. Again, carefully thump the plaster on the table to remove air bubbles. After it cools, use a small knife to dislodge the cast metal. If you have been careful, the mold should remain intact in case you have to make another pour. If the casting was successful, the student can now use small files, emery paper, and rouge on a buffing wheel to bring the item to conclusion.

I have also had students make fine castings in dry compacted sand, pieces of charcoal, and the old standby cuttlefish. The process is the same as above.

Another technique for casting is called "the lost wax method." The students sculpt a design with beeswax—carved in detailed by using dentist's tools. The wax is then coated in plaster (called investment), with a plastic drinking straw (sprue) placed in the wax and the plaster moulded around it. When dry, the straw is removed. The entire setup is placed in an oven or kiln and heated until the wax is totally burned out. It is then allowed to cool off.

Hot metal is poured into the cool mould through the funnel created by the straw. Immediately place the mould with the molten metal in a bucket and spin it in a wide circle from ground to ceiling at your side. A steady motion is more important than a fast or mighty swing. This centrifugal force will allow the hot metal to reach every detail within the mould. When completed, allow the mould and metal to cool, then break it open, and proceed to finish as stated previously.

Larger castings are also possible, but the instructions for doing this go beyond the scope of this book.

Engraving

I have had students engrave copper plate for bookmarks and knives from the smithy. The process is the same. First, clean the metal surface thoroughly with mineral spirits, dry it, and paint on a thin even coat of roofing tar (asphaltum), thinned with turpentine, over every part of the metal. When this is dry, take engraving tools and carefully etch a design that has been previously placed on paper. The etching will remove the tar and will expose the metal.

In a glass baking dish add the appropriate acid and place the metal in the bath. (For copper you would use one part nitric acid to one part water. Always add the acid to the water. For steel you would use two parts hydrochloric acid to one part water.) You will notice that the acid will bubble around the engravings. Use a feather to remove those bubbles that adhere to the metal. They will prevent the acid from reaching the metal and will cause an uneven bite.

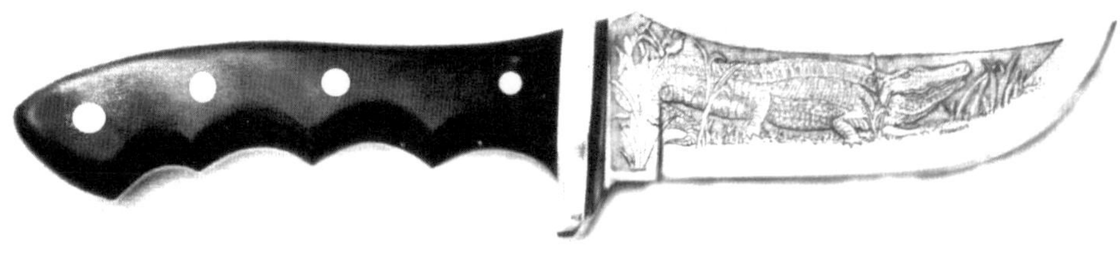

Knife engraved with alligator motif.

Allow the acid to work for ten minutes or so, and then remove the item from the bath, stop the acid action by dipping it in water, and carefully observe if the etching is deep enough for your satisfaction. The slower the bite the more even the engraving will be! Continue this until you are content. Then place the metal in a large pail of water to neutralize the acid. Finally, remove the excess tar with mineral spirits, and buff polish with red rouge and a soft cotton buffing wheel. Remember to use extreme caution when working with acid! Wear safety glasses, a protective apron, rubber gloves, and ensure that there is adequate ventilation.

Polishing metal

A polished appearance is the result of a perfectly flat and smooth surface. The students should always be encouraged to avoid making unnecessary marks on their metalwork. It is advisable to guide the students through each of the following steps, not allowing them to skip one.

- Use a file to smooth all edges or to define shapes.

- Use abrasive paper such as silicon carbide (wet/dry) paper. Begin with a coarse grit and work toward the finest, always rinsing the object in water to remove excess grit.

  50-100 grit paper is very coarse
  200s are coarse
  300s are medium
  400s are fine
  500s are very fine

- Use a soft cotton buffing wheel on either a hand cranked or electric buffing machine. Apply an oxide buffing compound to the moving wheel. Buff first with a coarse compound, then use a fine one. I have two buffing wheels set up, one for a coarse grit, the other for the final. Never mix grits on the same wheel.

Bobbing — a gray material which contains pumice. It is rough and good for the initial buff.
White — another fast cutting oxide

Diamond — a fast cutting compound with diamond dust in it

Tripoli — a fine brown compound that will remove scratches and give a nice polish

Red rouge — a fine delicate compound for the final polish (also called Jeweler's Rouge)

- Use #0000 steel wool on small jewelry and articles with a lot of edges.

Copperwork

Transforming a flat piece of sheet copper into a bowl with stroke after stroke of carefully aimed hammer blows, while at the same time spirally turning the copper is an exercise in dexterity. You have to work slowly and deliberately, always ensuring that the copper remains uniform in its thickness.

In the high school, bracelets, jars, vases, and ladles are made. The students learn that rhythm saves strength. Ten days of hammering are needed to make a vase. For twenty hours each stroke must be identical to the one before it in order to produce a beautiful form. Stamina is developed. Working with copper develops a feeling for form and space as well as rhythmical mobility.

Copper offers a great deal of resistance through its hardness. The chasing hammer acts as a mediator between the work-piece and hand. The student must consistently guide hammer blow beside hammer blow, beginning at the center and shifting up in a spirally moving pattern.

There are many ways of working copper. I will describe some that I have found effective.

Copper bowl making

• Using metal snips and a compass cut a circle from a piece of 20 to 16 gauge copper sheet.

• You must have a concavity. I have several stumps and in the middle of each I gouged and smoothed a depression in the end grain.

Place the copper disk across the center of the depression and tap it with a leather mallet. Work progressively from the circumference toward the center. Anneal the copper as needed.

• When you have achieved the desired depth, invert it and smooth out the surface over a rounded stake held in a vise with a planishing hammer. Work from the center to the periphery in a spiral pattern. Carefully, evenly spaced strokes will create a lovely dimpled surface that will throw the light and make it sparkle. A flat lump of lead will allow you to hammer special shapes into the copper, such as the bowl on the left.

Crimping

If you want to make a large bowl, you might wish to crimp the copper. Crimping is a technique in which you place radial folds in the copper sheet to help the forming.

- With a pencil, mark the disk into segments.
- Place the disk over a notched stake and with a cross-peen hammer make it fluted.
- Smooth the flutes with a planishing hammer over a rounded, polished post or a T-stake. Ensure that you always rise from the point of the crimp out to the edge.

Soldering

You will have to solder at some point. When a metal is heated, it will reach a temperature where the internal crystals move apart. Solder melts and flows into these gaps and creates a bond between surfaces.

I like to use silver solder because of its low melting temperature and relative ease of use.

- First, make sure that the pieces fit snugly, then clean the pieces to be soldered with emery paper or steel wool.
- Next apply flux.
- With a propane torch apply an even heat. All pieces must reach soldering temperature simultaneously.

- Remove the heat and apply the solder on the side opposite where you last applied the heat. Solder flows toward heat. Don't use an excess of solder, which will complicate the finishing of the piece.

A ladle, rings, bracelets, and small bowls are some of the objects that the students can make.

An example of copper chasing where a design is placed in the copper through the careful striking of the hammer upon a tool moving along a prescribed pattern.

Repoussé

This is an ancient process that gives shape to a sheet of metal by pressing it out from the back and in from the front.

- First draw the design on a piece of annealed copper.
- Prepare a pan of black pitch by heating it gently. Ensure proper ventilation.
- Lay the copper sheet on the pitch and go over the design with a tracer punch.
- Remove the metal carefully and soak it in a bath of mineral spirits or turpentine to remove the pitch which has adhered.
- Turn the metal over and set it back on the pitch. Boss up the form with a rounded tool or a popsicle stick.
- Remove when finished, clean, and buff with a liquid metal polish and a soft cloth.

Pitch can be purchased from Northwest Pitchworks, 5705 26th Ave., N.E. Seattle, Washington 98105.

Mythological face worked into thin sheet copper.

Blacksmithing

Blacksmithing in grades ten to twelve develops character as well as manual skill. Respect for the power of the red hot metal comes quickly to the aspiring blacksmith, but there is no time for timidity, because the metal has to be worked with spontaneity and focus. Life today is also fast-paced and demands immediacy. The worker must use his strength energetically, even explosively! There is no room for hesitation, because once the metal cools it loses its plasticity. The time is very short. The look on a student's face when she transforms a 3/4-inch square stock into a multiple twist pattern with relative ease is a sight to behold. Confidence is developed. The forge trains powers of decision. The blacksmith learns the fundamentals of the craft: keeping the forge fire burning, not allowing an oxidizing flame, handling the tools in a proper fashion, and developing an understanding for the laws of metallurgy.

Bruce Archer, a professor at the Royal College of Art, had an old great-aunt who, in the early nineteenth century, first wrote the catchy educational phrase that has come to be known as the three R's (reading, writing and 'rithmetic). This, his aunt maintained, was a misquotation of an earlier aphorism: "reading (and writing), reckoning (and figuring), and wroughting (and wrighting)." A young person's experience with wroughting, or blacksmithing, was considered to be an important foundation in the development of thinking.

Independence and self-reliance are the cornerstones of survival. Anyone wishing to achieve a degree of non-dependence should acquire at least some capability in blacksmithing. This lost art is making a revival throughout many Waldorf high schools around the world.

Why should we place emphasis on a skill that seems so irrelevant today? After all, how many people today ever require the services of a blacksmith?

By mastering blacksmithing you are able to create just about any tool you may need.

Setting up the Blacksmith Shop

by David Mitchell & Martin Kruse

The first thing to consider is a suitable workplace. The requirements are fairly simple. You need an area inside or out that has shade over the forge area. Direct sunlight makes it impossible to judge the color (thus, the temperature) of the metal. My shop is such that the students and I can work both outside and in, but of course this depends on local weather conditions. If you work inside, it is advisable to have a concrete floor, water, electricity, and fairly easy access to the outdoors. Remember that a forge produces a lot of carbon monoxide, which is poisonous, so make sure that you provide adequate ventilation. An extra wide door will provide proper ventilation for the smoke and dust to clear out. I also often have a window open.

The next consideration is what equipment to provide. The one item which you'll unquestionably be better off buying than attempting to make or improvise yourself is an anvil. The best ones weigh 150 pounds and up and come from England, Sweden, or Germany. It is possible to find used anvils in garage sales and farm auctions. Just be certain to look carefully at the table of the anvil to make sure it isn't damaged beyond repair. I have ground down and retempered several anvils, and they were better than new ones.

An anvil that is properly tempered will give a good lively bounce to your hammer. Working on a "dead" anvil is sheer drudgery. The anvil will require a stand on which it can be mounted solidly at a convenient working height. You can either make or select a suitable log butt. The table of the anvil should be at the knuckle height of the students using it. I take a length of chain, wrap it around the four bottom flanges of the anvil and bolt it to the log. This makes it solid. Then I take a length of military webbing and wrap and screw it to the circumference of the log to make loops to receive hammers and tongs.

A metal barrel filled with concrete and with some lead poured on top also works well to hold an anvil.

Next, you'll need a forge. Commercially made ones are available, but they've always seemed outrageously expensive to me. You may be able to find an old one in working condition at a decent price, or you can make your own.

I have three in my school shop. The first I built. I took a four-by-four-foot 1/4 -inch piece of steel. I welded 3-inch high sides around all four edges, cut a hole in the center for a firepot with a tuyre assembly, an adjustable air gate and a dumping ashgate, which I purchased from Centaur Forge, 117 North Spring St., Burlington, WI 53105-0340. I then purchased four screw flanges from our local hardware store, welded them to the bottom of the steel plate, and screwed in four, 30-inch long, $1^1/_2$-inch diameter pipes for the legs.

All forges achieve intense heat from air being forced through the fire. You need some form of blower. At a local secondhand store I purchased a used hair dryer to which I screw-clamped a $2^1/_2$-inch metal flexible hose. This provided forced air to the coal. This large forge will accommodate 6-8 students at one time, if they rotate between the anvil and the forge.

I also have a portable forge that will allow two to four students to work at it. It has a hand-cranked Buffalo blower and looks slightly like a backyard charcoal grill. In fact, I have friends who have made portable forges by lining a backyard grill with concrete to make a safe firepot.

Because smoke became a problem for my neighbors, I purchased a Quantum double burner propane gas forge to use when local weather conditions were not favorable for coal burning. This forge has the advantage of quickly reaching welding heat. It is economical in that it burns only two pounds of fuel per hour. It has a built-in blower that requires electricity.

Besides the forge, anvil, and blower you'll require several slake tubs. This is nothing more than 5-gallon plastic buckets. You will need to place these around your shop for cooling hot steel and for use in case of a small fire. I also fill one with sand for slow-cooling steel. One bucket, with a ladle, needs to be close to the coal fire for cooling it down and keeping the fire from spreading out from the center to the periphery and thus using more coal than necessary. A metal barrel filled with old motor oil for quenching is needed when you're tempering tool steel. It is critical that this be metal—anything else will catch fire—and you will have a mess on your hands.

Good sturdy workbenches are a must. It is easy to build these yourself if you're resourceful. I have one table that is all metal which I purchased for $10 from a government surplus center. You will also need several sturdy metal machinist's vises. I have six of these I bought for $15 each at a surplus center. I also have one blacksmith's post vise.

There are a few tools you will need to get started. After the first few are purchased, you can make almost all the others you need.

Tongs are used to hold the hot metal while you're working it. They come in an infinite number of sizes and shapes for different work. Most of the blacksmithing books advise that you can't have too many, and I know a few smiths who have racks of a hundred or more. I have about a dozen and it seems as if I use two at most. My favorite is a 15 $^{1}/_{2}$-inch Peddinghaus flat-nosed. I supplement the twenty pairs of tongs in my shop with many pairs of hand-held, adjustable, Vise Grips.

Hammers are what you need to actually shape and form the hot metal. Most smiths have at least a half-dozen which they'll tell you they can't get along without. I've probably got three dozen in my shop, and I use every one. They range in size from two ounces to eight pounds with a wide variety of shapes and faces, including a few that I had to make because they're not available commercially. The most useful hammers for general forging are in the range of one and a half to four pounds. Get some cross peens, double face, and ball peens, and a straight peen if you can find one. I get some light hammers for the young ladies.

I find it mandatory to have one steel-shafted, full sized, twelve-pound sledge with a steel handle to eliminate breakage.

You'll need to have some means of cutting metal. A hacksaw with a supply of blades is a necessity, and no shop should be without one, but, as you progress in your smithing ability, you'll find ways to avoid this form of drudgery. Cutting iron or steel is most easily done when it's hot. The simplest way of handling cutoff chores on rod or bar stock is with a hardy. This is a chisel-like tool that fits in the square hole in your anvil which, incidentally, is called the hardy hole. The red hot metal is cut by placing it on top of the hardy and striking it with the hammer. They're fairly simple to make, or you can buy a pretty good one for about $20. In addition, you may wish to obtain an assortment of hot cutter chisels, cold chisels, and maybe even a shear of some sort as you expand your operation.

You need some way to make holes. A good drill press will come in handy. I presently have a table-mounted Delta. In New Hampshire my shop had two hand-cranked post-mounted drill presses. These two jewels showed the children how the mechanical advantage was achieved through the gears and counter wheels.

You can put holes in metal by heating and punching. If you need a precise size hole, you may have to punch it undersized and ream it, but you can make all the punches and reamers you need without too much trouble. You can do all your wood drilling with a bit and brace if you have to. If your budget is a little tight or you feel ambitious, you can make these. The brace isn't too difficult, and wood boring bits are much simpler to make than steel cutting twist drills.

Taps and dies for cutting threads come in quite handy when you are assembling things. Making these is beyond the skills of most beginning smiths. Consider buying a few to get started.

You will need wire brushes and various files for fitting, finishing, final shaping, sharpening, and a million other things. It would be possible to write a book just on types of files and their uses. I do not believe it's possible for a shop to have too many of them. They are difficult, tedious, and time-consuming to make by hand. As long as they're commercially available, consider it money well spent and buy a bunch. An excellent book on files—how to maintain them, use them, distinguish the main use of each, and so forth, can be obtained by writing to Nicholson File Company in Providence, Rhode Island, and asking for their free publication ***File Philosophy***.

A grinder, like the drill press, is a necessity. Gear-driven, hand-cranked grinders are still made and are available through many catalogues such as Woodcraft Supply in Massachusetts. They feature a few hand-cranked wet wheels which use aluminum oxide grinding wheels. At one time just about every smithy, even small barnyard operations, had one of the old treadle powered sandstone grinding wheels which ran either in a water tray or with a drip funnel. If you can find one of these today, consider yourself fortunate. If the stone itself is in good shape and the price is reasonable, grab it. You can rebuild the rest of the mechanism yourself.

That covers the basics for setting up a shop in your Waldorf school. Of course, there are still a couple hundred odds and ends (fullers, flatters, swage blocks, mandrels, and so forth) that you'll want later. You might want an apron. If so be sure to get one made out of mule skin—this is heavier and safer then any other. The list of items you can purchase can fill pages. What we've discussed here should be more than adequate to get started, and you're probably better off waiting to acquire the rest until you've had a little experience. Hammer some hot metal, read a few books, look over the equipment catalogs, then hammer some more. Then you'll be able to make informed decisions as to what else you need.

I strongly recommend ***The Complete Metalsmith*** by Tim McCreight, Davis Publications, ISBN 0-87192-240-1. This is by far the finest practical handbook on working with all types of metals that I have come across.

Steel Designations and Composition

Number	Description
10xx	Plain C
11xx	Resulphurized C
13xx	Mn 1.75%
23xx	Ni 3.50%
25xx	NI 5.00%
31xx	Ni 1.25%, Cr 0.65-0.80%
33xx	NI 3.50%, Cr 1.55%
40xx	Mo 0.25%
41xx	Cr 0.95%, Mo 0.20%
43xx	Ni 1.80%, Cr 0.50-0.80%, Mo 0.25%
46xx	NI 1.80%, Mo 0.25%
48xx	Ni 3.50%, Mo 0.25%
50xx	Cr 0.30%, or 0.60%
51xx	Cr 0.80%, 0.95% or 1.05%
5xxxx	C 1.00%, Cr 0.50%, 1.00% or 1.45%
61xx	Cr 0.80% or 0.95%
86xx	NI 0.55%, Cr 0.50%, Mo 0.20%
87xx	Ni 0.55%, Cr 0.50%, Mo 0.25%
92xx	Mn 0.85%, A 2.00%
93xx	NI 3.25%, Cr 1.20%, Mo 0.12%
94xx	Mn 1.00%, Ni 0.45%, Cr 0.40%, Mo 0.12%
97xx	Ni 0.55%, Cr 0.17%, Mo 0.20%
98xx	NI 1.00%, Cr 0.80%, Mo 0.25%

C = Carbon Cr = Chromium Mn = Manganese

Si = Silicon Ni = Nickel

xx In the last two places, this designates the points of carbon in the steel.

These designations are used by the American Iron and Steel Institute and the Society of Automotive Engineers.

How to Temper Steel

by David Mitchell & Martin Kruse

The art of tempering steel is a precise one, and one that must be learned if you are to make serviceable items. Tempering makes the edge last longer, the punch harder and more accurate, and all tools more serviceable.

First obtain a magnet with a long handle (or one you can hold onto with a pair of tongs). When the steel starts getting up to red hot, check it frequently with the magnet. When the magnet doesn't stick, the steel is hot enough. Remember that the hardening step must be accomplished uniformly for the entire tool. Make sure that the entire piece is at cherry red. If you're working with a very large or thick piece of steel, you'll need to let it "soak" in the heat to make sure it's heated all the way through. You probably had the air going pretty near full blast to get the work up to this heat. Now slow down the air flow and let things sit at a nice even heat for a couple of minutes. (If you're using a hand cranked blower, this is fairly simple. If you have an electric blower, you'll need to dampen your airgate to gain control over your airflow. Installing a butterfly valve might also suffice, but the best bet is a speed control switch on the blower motor. This is an in-line type switch and extremely simple to install. If you don't already have one, we highly recommend the investment of the $20 or so they cost. You'll find the added control over the fire makes all of your work at the forge easier. Getting the right temperature is the critical factor in the hardening step. If you don't get it hot enough, the steel either won't reach full hardness, or it won't harden at all. If it's not heated through fully, you might only obtain hardening on the surface.

Any of these conditions (especially the last two) will make it impossible to temper the work properly. If you have inadequate heat resulting in any of these conditions, you'll need to repeat the hardening step. As I said, hardening is the simple part, but there are still certain tricks that can save you grief.

First, you'll impart less shock to the steel and be a lot less likely to have the piece crack if you pre-heat the oil (most bladesmiths seem to agree on a temperature between 150 and 200 degrees). To do this, simply take a piece of steel (mild steel or any scrap you have around will do fine) and heat it up and drop it in the quenching tub. How large a piece and how hot you need it to be will depend on the size of the tub and how cold the oil is to begin with. I use a large coffee can in my school shop. A professional's tub is a little over twenty gallons. With this, two four-inch squares of one quarter-inch plate heated red hot and dropped in usually do the trick. You can check by sticking a finger in the oil, and if it's hot enough to be uncomfortable, it's about right. If you're new at this, though, I suggest you get a thermometer. Blacksmiths tend to have heat-insensitive hands. What may be uncomfortably hot to a seasoned blacksmith's hands can raise blisters on a beginner. If you've got it all together now, you should have a good, deep, even fire going, and your oil is heated, so put your tool to be hardened in the fire. A good deep reducing fire is highly desirable here, as this will minimize oxidation and decarbonization, i.e., you'll have less surface pitting that will have to be ground and polished after heat treating. Remember that, any time you are working with high carbon steel. Use the cleanest burning fuel you can get and try to maintain a clean fire. Bring the steel up to the decalescence point (about fifteen hundred degrees Fahrenheit), checking it with a magnet. When it reaches the proper heat, grab it with a pair of long-handled tongs, take it out of the fire, and immerse it in oil. Hold onto it. Don't just drop the piece in the oil tub. Hold it about midway down in the oil. If you bump the side or bottom of the can or barrel, your piece will warp or twist. You'll probably get a flash ignition fire on the surface of the oil. Get the hot metal down into it fast, and this will go out. (It's a good idea to have a cover handy for your oil tub, just in case.) Hold the piece in the oil until it's cooled enough to hold in your hand. Allow the excess oil to drip back into the can, and carefully wipe the item with a disposable paper towel. At this point, if everything went right, the steel is at its full hardness. Check it with a file. If you've obtained full hardness on #5160 steel, a dull file won't touch it. A new sharp file will just barely bite.

Assuming that things are going properly, you now have a tool which is so hard that it would be almost impossible to sharpen and is much too brittle to stand up to any severe use. You need to temper it. At this point, if you used a petroleum based oil, the piece is probably about as black and grungy as an automobile oil pan after an engine fire. This is all right, except you won't be able to see the temper colors run under all the burned-on carbon. So, first you need to clean it off.

If you do not have a belt grinder, some 220-grit emery cloth and a lot of elbow grease will do the trick. (A very important word of caution here. If you do use any type of power equipment on the hardened or tempered steel, you MUST take precautions against getting the steel hot. If it starts to turn colors during grinding, you are ruining the temper. I run a water drip on my grinder belt and do all of my grinding after hardening without gloves, so that I can feel any heat build up in the steel, before it is too late.

Once you have a clean, bright metal surface, you're ready for the tricky part, tempering. In order to "draw temper," you need to reheat the steel. You're not exactly softening it, but you are removing some of the hardness in order to attain a suitable degree of toughness for the tool's intended use.

Tempering takes place at temperatures between 450 and 700 degrees Fahrenheit for the types of steel you're most likely to be dealing with. The two factors that determine the hardness are the carbon content of the steel and the temperature which you heat it to. Let's assume you already know the carbon content; therefore, the key to achieving the desired results is determining the temperature. You do this by eye. As steel heats up, a mild oxidation process causes the surface to change color several times as it gets hotter. The color of the steel indicates the temperature and, thereby, the point to which the temper has drawn. The steel will run through a series of changes from light straw color to darker straw to bronze to purple to dark blue to lighter shades of blue down to a sky blue.

It may take you a little while to get accustomed to judging the color. Just remember that it gets easier after you've done it a few times and that you should try to achieve fairly consistent lighting conditions from one working session to the next.

You must have subdued light or shade. Any direct light, especially direct sunlight, coming into your forge will make it all but impossible to make an accurate eyeball determination of the steel's temperature. A lot of smiths do their heat -treating in the morning, because the light seems to be best for it during this part of the day.

For any tool, sky blue is as far as you'll ever want to let it run. The following charts should help you determine the temper you want for different tools. When it reaches the desired point, you halt the process by quenching it.

You can make tools that will outperform and outlast factory-made products. This is achieved through what is called a differential temper. Now we get to the tricky stuff. First, let me back up a minute and explain what this is and why it's so desirable. Then we'll get to how to do it.

Think about it, and you'll see that different parts of a tool actually perform different functions and have to stand up to different types of stress. A simple illustration of this is a tool such as a cold chisel. The edge must be very hard (light straw) but the back end must have the ductility to withstand repeated hammer blows, requiring that the temper be drawn much further in this area (perhaps even all the way to light blue depending on the steel used).

Punches and drifts are other examples of tools in this category that require this particular type of temper. A knife is much more complex. For example, if the edge is too hard, it will be difficult to sharpen and will chip easily, but it must be hard enough to take and hold a keen cutting edge. The back must withstand some shock from chopping or even being pounded on, and the tang must stand up to the brunt of the shock when it is used for chopping and also stand the torque and strain when someone misuses it as a pry-bar.

Depending on the size and type of knife and the type of steel used, I might, for example, draw the edge to a bronze or deep purple, with the back correspondingly a purple or dark blue. The tangs are drawn to sky blue. Accomplishing this can be a little tricky, because the places where you want to draw the least temper are almost always the thinnest, which means that they heat up fastest (just what you don't want). You need to heat the piece unevenly.

There are several techniques for doing this. In the case of the center punch, it's fairly easy. Stick the back end in the fire and watch the temper colors run down toward the point. If you're really lucky and everything works just right, the back will be the shade of blue you want when the point turns straw. Then you can quench the whole thing, and you're set. But nobody gets that lucky the first time (probably because it's seldom really luck but more often a lot of experience and knowing how to control the fire). What's more likely is that either one of two things will happen. Either the point will reach straw color and the back won't have reached the desired shade of blue, or the back will reach light blue and the point won't have turned color at all.

You can halt the process in one part of the tool by immersing one end of the tool in the oil. Holding it this way will allow the temper to run down the remainder. When it reaches the desired stage, submerge the entire piece.

Another technique is to wrap part of the tool in wire and pack clay around it. Now this part will not have as much heat as the exposed tool face. Experiment a bit, and you will find the technique that works best for you.

That's how the process works. Other tools such as froes, adzes, and ax heads are a little more involved.

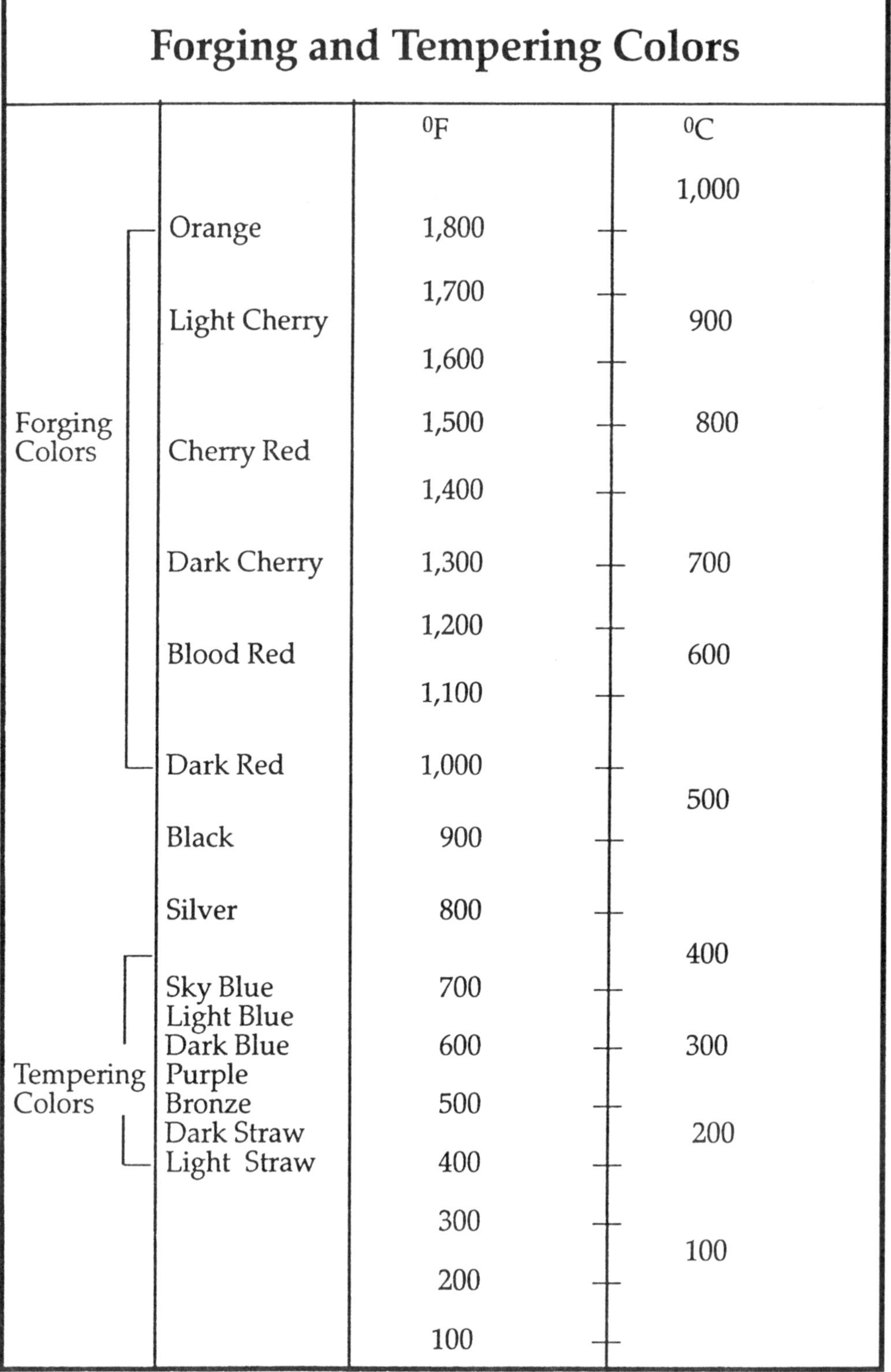

Forging and Tempering Colors

		^{0}F	^{0}C
			1,000
	Orange	1,800	
		1,700	
	Light Cherry		900
		1,600	
		1,500	800
Forging Colors	Cherry Red		
		1,400	
	Dark Cherry	1,300	700
		1,200	
	Blood Red		600
		1,100	
	Dark Red	1,000	
			500
	Black	900	
	Silver	800	
			400
	Sky Blue	700	
	Light Blue		
	Dark Blue	600	300
Tempering Colors	Purple		
	Bronze	500	
	Dark Straw		200
	Light Straw	400	
		300	
			100
		200	
		100	

Summary : Annealing, hardening, and tempering

Steel is most workable (easiest to drill, file, grind or cut) when it has been annealed. Annealing is the process of heating steel red hot and cooling it very slowly (in the air or in a bucket of dry sand). To anneal copper you cool it quickly in a bucket of water.

Heat treating is a two step process, hardening and tempering. In hardening, the steel is put into the fire and brought to a critical temperature (called the decalesence point). This point is usually cherry red. When the steel reaches this point, it becomes nonmagnetic.

Hardening – heat steel to red, then dip in oil bath

Tempering – draw the edge to a bronze or deep purple
draw the back to a purple or dark blue
draw the tang to a sky blue

At each stage dip in an oil bath.

Blacksmithing projects

The introduction to blacksmithing involves learning the basic skills of shaping hot steel. I like to begin with a simple hook. The first step is to cut off a 7-inch piece of $^1/_4$-inch square stock and heat one end in the fire until it glows red. With a two-pound hammer successive strokes are applied to one end until an even taper results. When the steel loses its color it must return to the fire. Hammering cold steel will splinter it.

The taper is heated once again and carefully it is bent over to make a lip. Then the reversed hook is formed over the horn of the anvil. The shank is heated, placed in a

The first hook is for a horse saddle; the others are decorative.

vise, and twisted with a crescent wrench. The students are always amazed at the malleability of the hot steel. Finally, the end is flattened by pounding it with a two-pound ball peen hammer, and a hole is punched or drilled to accept a screw for mounting it onto wall. The final step is to wirebrush the hook to a dark, even shine.

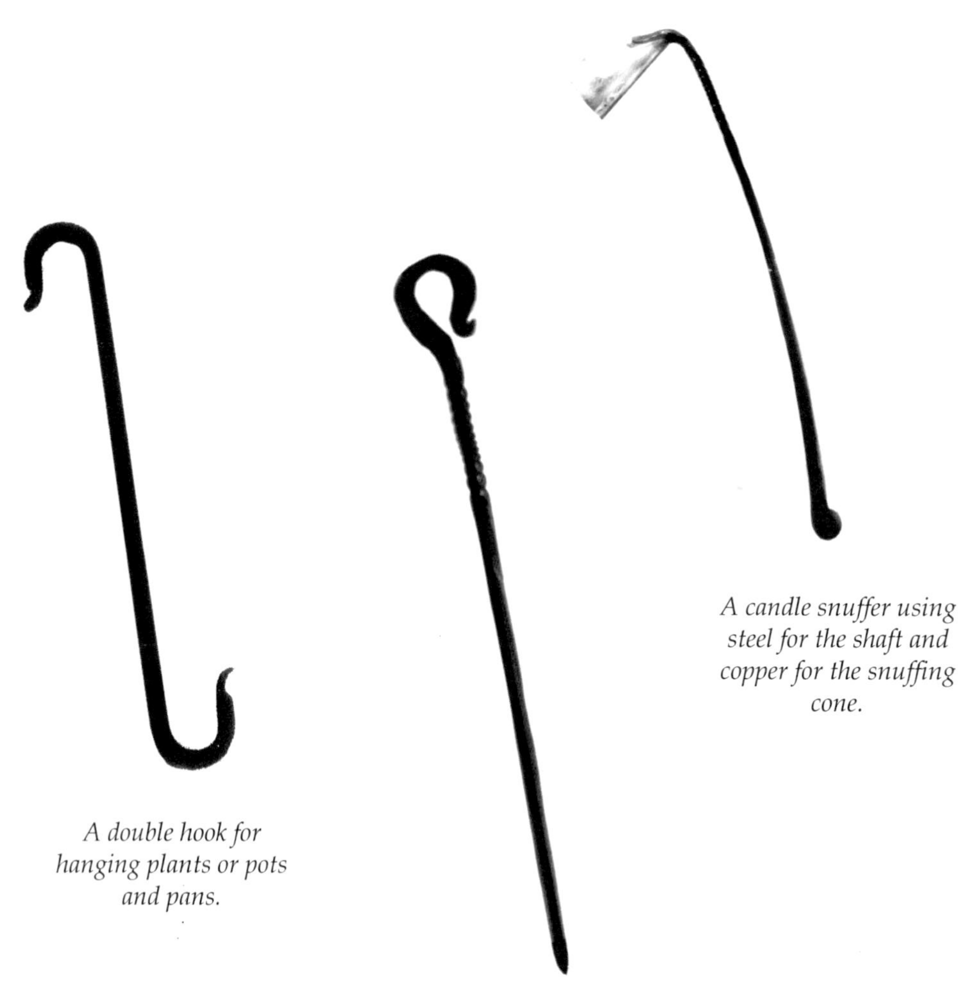

A candle snuffer using steel for the shaft and copper for the snuffing cone.

A double hook for hanging plants or pots and pans.

A cooking point for shishksbob.

Bladesmithing

The art of making the most basic of all tools—a knife—involves a detailed process of design with function in mind. The next step takes you to the forge where the steel is hammered into a rough shape. Then it is filed with a bastard file, ground on an abrasive wheel or knifemaker's grinder. When the proper angles are concavely cut, the long process of polishing the blade, setting the temper, as well as making the tang, handle, and sheath ensues. All of this requires concentration, stamina, a high degree of perfection, and strict attention to safety.

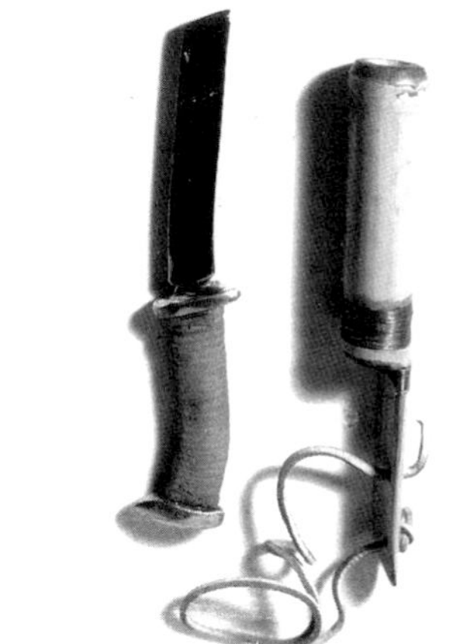

A tanto with bamboo sheath.

A Bowie with a leather sheath.

An assortment of blades.

Knives with antler handles.

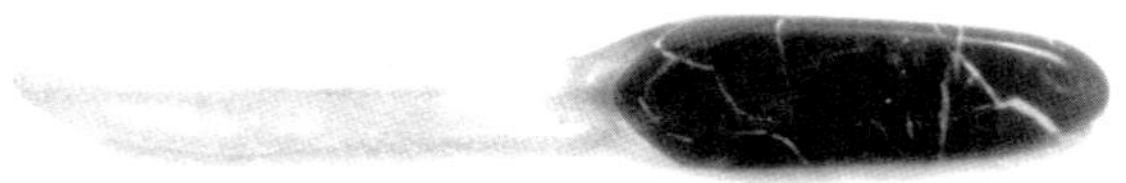

A two-sided blade with a marble handle.

Stonecarving

by David Mitchell

Life is pure adventure, and the quicker we realize that, the quicker we will be able to treat life as art; to bring all our energies to each encounter, to remain flexible enough to notice and admit when what we expected to happen did not happen. We need to remember that we are created creative and can invent new scenarios as frequently as they are needed.

– Maya Angelou

In the twelfth grade, when their high school career is coming to a close, the seniors have a main lesson block where they study Faust by Goethe. This block leads them into discussions about the nature of the human being. At the same time, in the practical arts, they are engaged in the carving of a life-sized human bust out of a rough chunk of stone. Carving stone is slow, strenuous work. It is like taking a wonderful and difficult journey as you search for the beauty hidden deep within the stone.

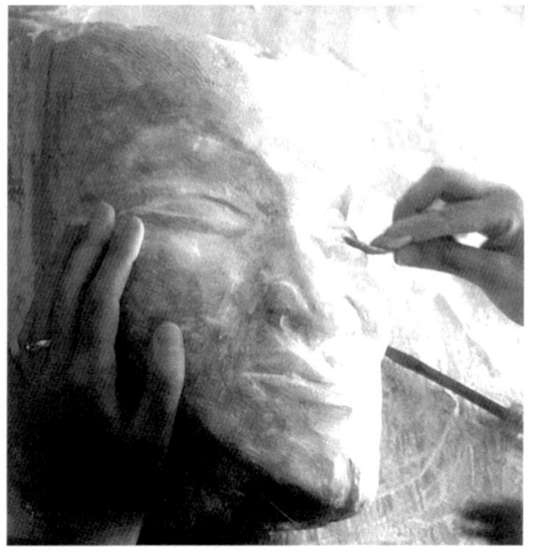

The stone used can be alabaster, marble, sandstone, soapstone, limestone or even granite (for the cholerics). The harder stones require a carbide centered point. However, the tools to work the other softer stones can easily be made in your blacksmith shop. Find several lengths of hardened 3/4-inch tool stock. Cut them into seven-inch lengths, grind points, set the temper and harden them.

I teach the following five techniques to my students:

1. Fracturing – breaking large chunks with a hatchet or point to reduce the stone's mass;
2. Chipping – breaking away small pieces of stone with a point;
3. Flaking – breaking thin layers along the grain of the stone;
4. Flattening – using the comb or flat chisel to bring the stone into a plane;
5. Pulverizing – using a bush hammer or carbide point to reduce the stone's surface to a powdery, granular material that blows away.

Safety is always the first concern. Students must wear protective eye glasses, suitable clothing, and footwear, and common sense must be used at all times. The studio should have an appropriate first aid kit.

After the students have selected their stones, they take their sharp point and a two-pound hammer and begin by pounding the stone gently on every face to find the grain and to experiment with the stone's individual texture.

Next, I have them place their stone on a pedestal and walk around it, observing carefully each face until they feel comfortable about how they will address the stone. Once satisfied, they take a piece of colored chalk and crudely draw the nose, chin, eyes, and forehead. Bags of sand are present and are used to prop the stone in the best position for carving.

With courage in hand they begin to chip away at the stone, reducing the face so that the nose will protrude. Then they carefully develop the eye sockets, the lips, and the chin. It is important, at this stage, to work all around the stone and not try to develop any one area to perfection.

At some point everyone will hit what I call the "eye of the needle." This is when they look at what they are doing and recognize it doesn't look like what they imagined it should, and they become frustrated. They may want to quit. They may even want to smash it with their hammer.

This is the time for the teacher to gently suggest that they become inwardly quiet and try to observe what the stone is trying to tell them. They must put aside any details they may have conjured up about how the stone should look. Their imposed, preconceived idea is now of no use. If they can do this, they will pass through the "eye of the needle" and may have a true artistic/creative experience.

Once the stone roughly resembles a human head, they take the comb-chisel and develop smoother planes. Following this they take the flat chisel and do the same to areas requiring smoothness.

Now comes the time for details, as they carefully form the eye and the upper lid. Placing a slight concavity under the eye makes it stand out more distinctly. The mouth also requires care. Observing each other, they will notice that the upper lip extends over the sides of the lower, but the lower is often the most extended. Some will be successful working with bastard files or "four in hands." Others will prefer to use riffler files, while still others will make their own tools out of sharpened spikes.

Harder stones will now require that they be worked with carbide stones of varying grits.

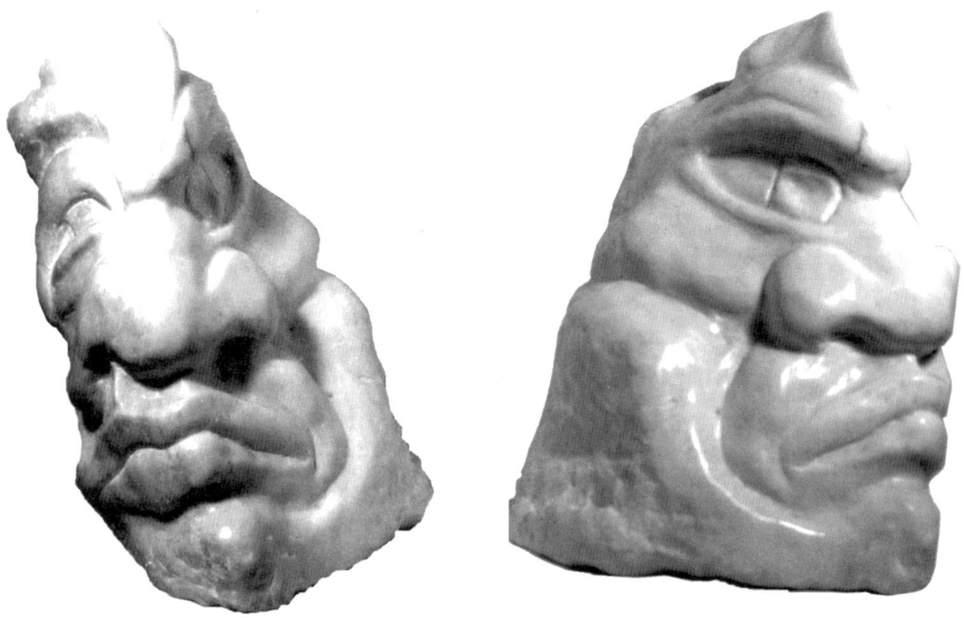

The students find interesting faces, even in the oddest shapes of marble.

The final stage consists of rubbing with wet and dry sandpaper of varying grits, water, and lots of elbow grease. Once smooth, the stone is carefully washed in running water, dried, and spray sealed with a clear lacquer.

Finally, the students polish their stones with four or five coats of beeswax or a paste floor wax, which is buffed wiith a soft cloth until the stones glisten.

A great deal of satisfaction arises out of the completed piece of artwork!

How do the experiences in stonecarving relate to cognitive development and other disciplines in the high school? A student, challenged by an English assignment asking him to write a descriptive essay about the process of artistic creation, drew from his Waldorf experiences and wrote the following essay:

Going through the Eye of the Needle

The early morning sun pierced through the studio windows creating long columns of light in the dusty air. Veiled by a white film, a large oak table commanded the center of the room. On it were a collection of hammers, points, comb chisels, rasps, and polishing stones. Lined like soldiers one next to the other, stone carvings stood at attention along the shelves hanging on the white lazured walls. Lions, noble heads, female busts, and numerous Henry Moore-inspired shapes peeked out from the once anonymous stones. Observing with a concentrated brow, his legs crossed, and strong gnarled hands clasped, sat the creator of these metamorphosed forms. His mind transfixed in an ethereal state, his strong, sinewy hands betrayed many years of toil; he pondered something far away.

Startled from his morning meditation by the bellow of a delivery truck horn, the sculptor rose to accept his prized medium of creation. Straining under the weight of the alabaster, he shuffled across the studio thumping the rock upon wooden stump. With a glimmer of both satisfaction and anticipation in his eye, he slowly paced around his prize examining every face with controlled intensity. The stone shown brilliantly, with every face impregnated with varied colors and shapes. He felt inspiration swell within him. Closing his eyes and running his hands over the irregular face of the stone, he wove his imagination into the contours and grain of the rock. His thoughts shaped the stone while the stone in turn shaped his thoughts. The end result revealed something new about each other. He began to see how a transformation could take place.

Gripping a two-pound hammer and a point chisel, he began to work the periphery of the alabaster slowly and carefully, chipping away small pieces with calculated strokes. He allowed the stone to help him understand its grain and hidden subtleties.

Next he took a piece of chalk and drew a vague image onto the stone. Stone pieces flew as the rhythmic staccato of the point and hammer brought forth three different planes into focus. In the play between concavity and convexity appeared a nose, a chin, and a forehead.

Suddenly he stopped. A look of dissatisfaction came upon his face. He retreated, looking intently at the stone from a distance. His knuckles whitened as the grip on his hammer intensified. He had come to the eye of the needle. His preconceived ideas were not being realized. Should he quit? No, the stone held the answer. He must let go of his intentions and work with his medium, allowing it to guide him in its own creation. He had passed this way before and knew that this was a true, artistic, creative moment.

With renewed inner vigor, and an observant eye, he returned to the stone from Utah. Applying the accuracy of a surgeon, he picked up the comb chisel and guided every blow toward a refinement of the shared image from his mind's eye and the stone's intentions. The whole stone was carved in totality; no one area was brought first to completion. The image slowly crawled forth from its rocky cocoon as its stately features became evident. Switching tools, a flat chisel refined the jagged contours, followed by a rasp, which further smoothed the cheeks and forehead. A smile of satisfaction swept across his face as he sealed the rock face and polished it to a high gloss with beeswax. The identity of the stone had emerged.

The bust shone brilliantly. Its noble complexion and piercing gaze caused one to stand in awe and amazement as if it were imbued with life itself. The stone had been true to him and had guided him past his imposing intentions. Creation had occurred in that sun drenched dusty room.

– N.A.M. (Student)
(used with permission)

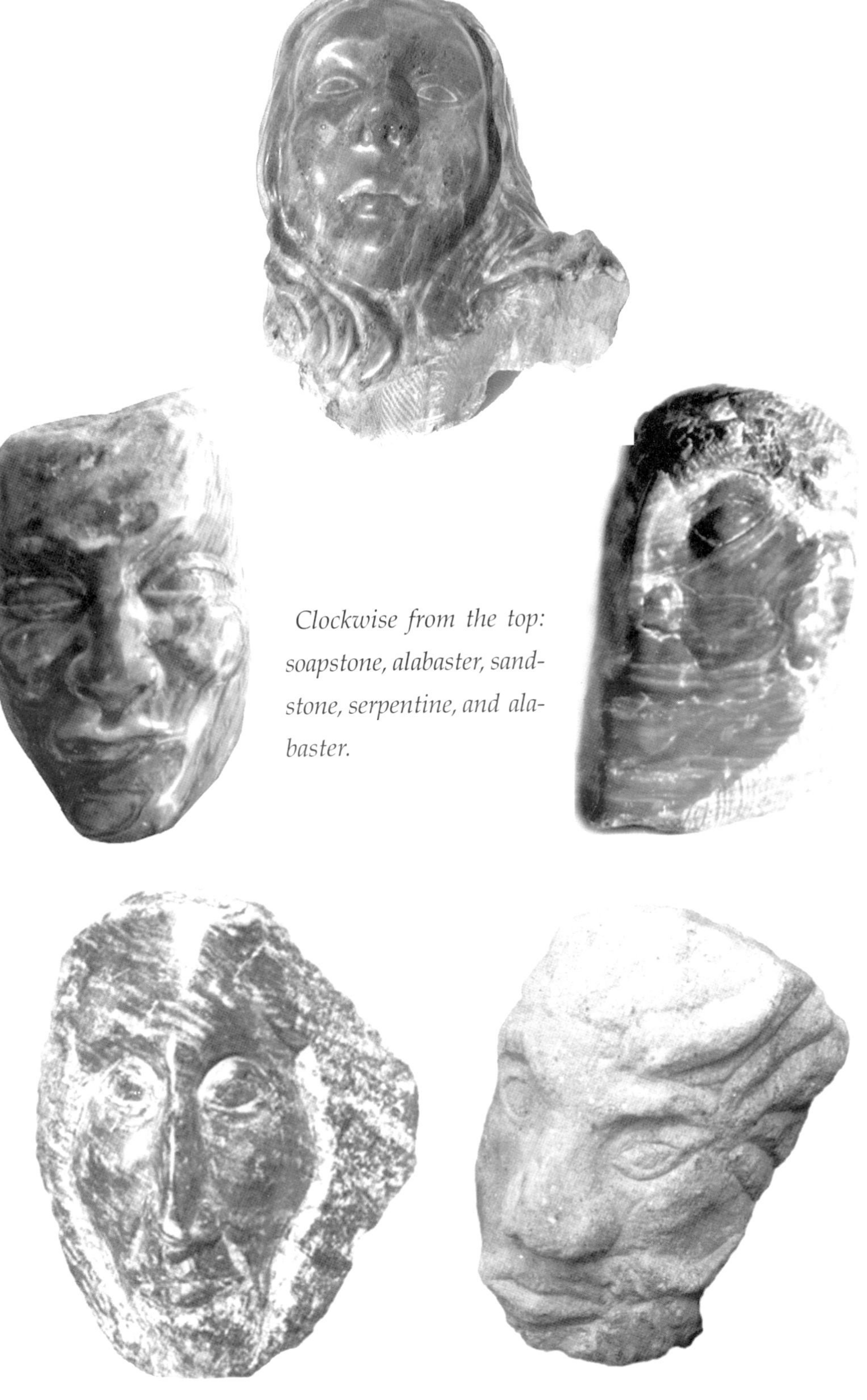

Clockwise from the top: soapstone, alabaster, sandstone, serpentine, and alabaster.

22

From Nature to Abstract Thinking: the Role of True Work

by
Michael Martin

Students need to understand, in a new way, all that surrounds them in the world. Everything that man himself has created through the observation of nature and the recognition of its laws should be penetrated with comprehension. Technology has issued from such comprehension. Rudolf Steiner considered it absolutely essential that each man, who, for example, uses a streetcar, know what happens technically so that he really understands how such motion can be accomplished.

> *We are living in the midst of a world produced by man, formed by human thoughts, which we use, and which we don't understand. This fact, that we understand nothing of something which is formed by man, of something which is basically the result of human thoughts, has great significance for the entire sphere in which the human soul and spirit live. . . . The worst is experiencing a world made by man, without concerning oneself with it in the slightest.*
>
> – Rudolf Steiner – ***The Study of Man***

Rudolf Steiner wanted the immediate experience of life to be brought to the schoolchildren. He considered this so important that he requested that a new subject be taught in the tenth grade: "Practical Life Studies" (*Lebenskunde*) which, among other things, was to include practical mechanics, spinning, weaving, soap making, and surveying. He explained repeatedly that the Greeks would never have come up with the idea of acquainting the youth with Egyptian culture, but rather allowed them to take part in the cultural stream of their own time. Shortly before the founding of the first Waldorf school in 1919 he said:

> *Beginning about the fourteenth or fifteenth year, when the delicately vibrating sentient soul comes into being, human beings ought to be introduced into the most immediate of present-day life instead of having their gaze deflected towards ancient cultural epochs, which received their structure under completely different social conditions.*

Naturally, this culmination of the subject "Lebenskunde" in the tenth grade has been prepared for a long time. From sixth grade on, the motif of work becomes an incisive experience through gardening and practical work in a real shop. Through taking hold of all that is to be experienced in inorganic nature, as in dynamics, statics, mechanics, mineralogy, and inorganic chemistry, the child of this age receives new and ample nourishment for the understanding of world interrelationships. Thus, the child's "arrival" on the earth comes about gradually, accompanied by an inclination toward heaviness and by the often awkward limb movements; both are direct consequences of a necessary developmental step. The young person turns inward and can be hard to decipher. Unlike the bubbling youth full of expression, the adolescent holds back his outer expression, saving something for himself; he senses a new inner space which can absorb and begin to digest what is moving him. Here also Rudolf Steiner helps us with the indication that now the personal destiny of the youth begins to work in him. The illuminated time of childhood has passed; the newly forming inner space is still dark. However, there lies a spark within it which can and should, through inner effort and strength, first spread brightness into that space and later radiate out more and more into the surrounding world. Again, it is true work and understanding which are the chief aids in gradually bringing about the proper relationship between that "inner" and "outer" space. This, seen from a social-human point of view, is now one of the main tasks in the upper grades.

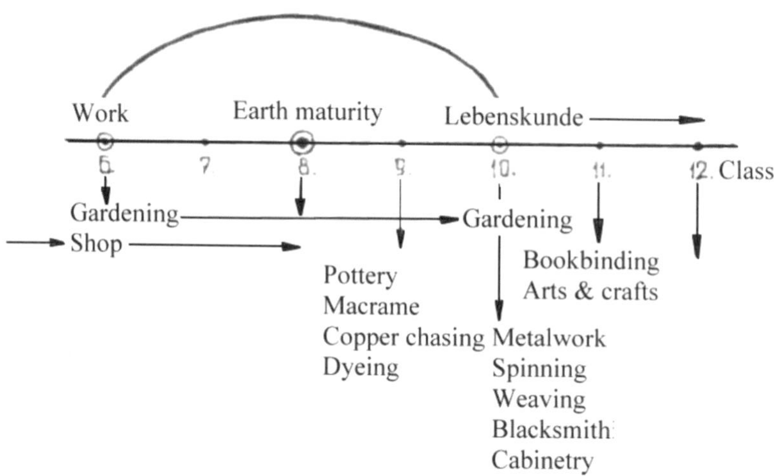

What has been sketched thus far are the low bass tones, the accompanying voices, the beat and the keys on which the melodies of the symphony depend and from which the harmony unfolds. We hear mostly only the upper sequence of melodies if we do not consciously take pains to grasp the fundamental musical elements as well. As teachers and parents in the pedagogical realm we are, of course, obliged to do just this. Which melodic sequences then rise out of the scaffolding we described? In the following, the handwork subjects are characterized as they were arranged in our high school. To this end only one point of view has been chosen, namely that of the *giving of form* to the youth.

Gardening is the only subject that leads straight through from the time of pre-maturity directly into the tenth grade. It should lead through from the preparatory cultivating work on the plant world to an overview of greater relationships (including an understanding of compost preparation, knowledge of the different soils, and the weather) and ultimately to more direct human intervention in natural relationships of growth processes through cultivation and refinement of fruit trees (grafting).

Whoever has turned a plot of hard ground, spent hours with bent back gathering potatoes from the field, or fastened wheat sheaves by hand in the burning sun, may well think of the angel who directed Adam to the earth with the harsh words: "In the sweat of thy brow shalt thou eat thy bread . . . ." and at the same time spoke of sorrow, thorns, and thistles which the earth and fields would bring him. Is this an image for the stage of development of the children, if from sixth grade on they are now to turn themselves to the earth in a very real way and only through toil and effort manage to coax life from her, like a presentiment of the tasks of life facing the adult? The paradise which, like a protecting mother, has nurtured us is lost:

> *One can say without exaggeration, for it is the truth: with puberty man is cast out of the spirit-soul life of the world and thrown into the outer world . . . .*
>
> – Rudolf Steiner

But, this being "cast out" contains within it a wonderful hope, like a bequest, a kind of continuation of paradise on earth. The plants, which maintain our bodily life, grow even today in connection with the cosmos, out of their own force. We human beings do not make the plants grow; but we can observe their germinating, sprouting, unfolding, withering, and new-becoming when we prepare the right soil out of our experience of their laws, when we care for the necessary moisture, for air, for sun and for the right warmth, while there is still danger of frost in the spring. All this the children experience more or less unconsciously in gardening. When we help the elements of earth, air, water, light, and warmth through working, caring, providing, and protecting, a bit of paradise can unfold around us which maintains our life through the nourishing plants and quickens our soul from year to year through the bounty of different varieties and blossoms.

At the same time, when we occupy ourselves with plants, we unite ourselves with earth and cosmos in yet another way, namely through their formative forces. Already from superficial observation we know the cups of the manifold blossoms which open up toward the light. Looking closer we discover that the green deciduous trees also turn toward the sun. Every single leaf of a tree is like an organ which longs for the light and reaches toward it. How great, however, is our astonishment when we discover that even the branches of the trees reach out like arms to the light. Together they also form vessels that open to the above. We can see this particularly well in the young shoots at the top of spruce and pine trees, which only later turn their branches to the earth as they get older and hang down through their own weight.

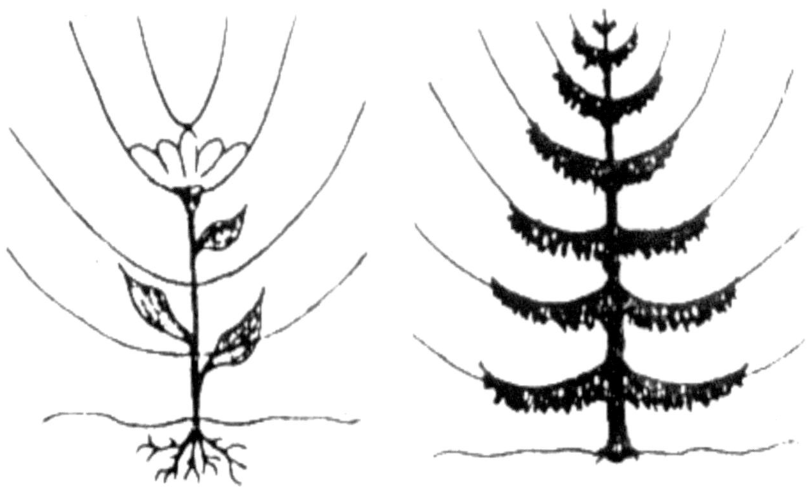

According to their form tendencies, plants are vessels turned toward the cosmos, parabolic forms which have their center in the sun. These "vessels" unfold out of the seed which rests in the earth. First a vertical, stretched-out, support-giving structure is formed—the stalk. On it the leaves begin to appear in a spiral which unfolds further and further toward the circumference, according to the species. Goethe, the untiring observer, called attention to these formative forces: "The two main tendencies, or if one wishes, the two living systems by which growing plant life fulfills itself are the vertical and the spiral systems; neither can be considered separately from the other because one grows only through the other" (***Concerning the Spiral Tendency of Vegetation***, 1831).

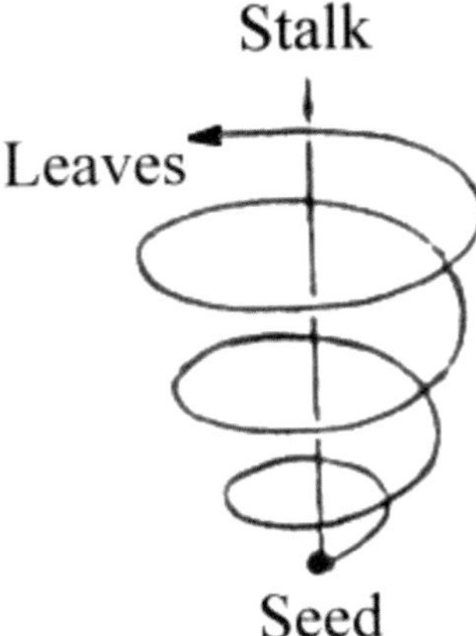

Now let us go down the steps from the garden into the pottery shop. It is located in the cellar, which is good because a certain amount of moisture is advantageous, and sunlight hinders the work. We take a lump of clay, big enough to fit into our hands. It feels cool and heavy. The moisture makes it so supple that it may easily be formed into a ball with the hollow surfaces of our hands. Keeping the clay in our hands, we press a hole into it with both thumbs and then round it off by turning it evenly. Thus, the tips of our thumbs press against the palms of our hands from inside, and with persistent turning and helical, climbing pressure a cavity is slowly formed; a vessel appears. Now it is set down and thus gets its flat bottom surface. A ring-like thicker bulge is added to the rim and is again formed from inside through turning and spiral-like pressure. The bowl grows. Now the direction of above/below must be experienced inwardly as a vertical shaft, so that the hollow space around this axis can grow in its circumference and not lose its direction and support. Otherwise the vessel will be crooked.

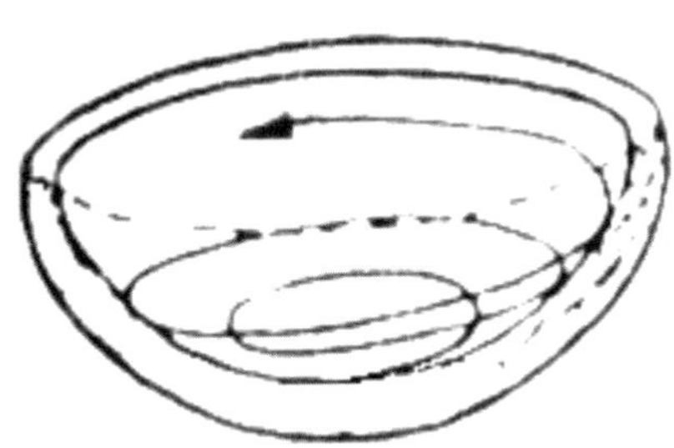

We have long since noticed that this technique was related to the growth of the plant, and, so to speak, almost as if it were "learned" from it. We find the same formative elements in both. Do we then still believe in the "theories of chance" which are imputed to all early technical inventions? It is generally known that men in primeval times were intimately connected with nature. Might they not have experienced the formative forces present in nature and then made use of this experience?

An extraordinary phase in the forming of a vessel begins when it is to get narrower again at the top or even to be almost closed. With this the actual forming of the hollow inner space truly begins. For some students this process is difficult to achieve. Intense inner concentration and mastering of any diversions from outer influences are necessary. The whole process of formation is dependent on the proper preparation of the clay, on its mixture of various complementary clays, on the right moisture. But also, after the actual forming of the vessel, the elements of air and warmth play a decisive role in drying and baking it. Even though the potter forms his vessels himself, the completion of his endeavors depends on the delicate interaction of the elements: earth, water, air, and warmth. This he still has in common with the gardener.

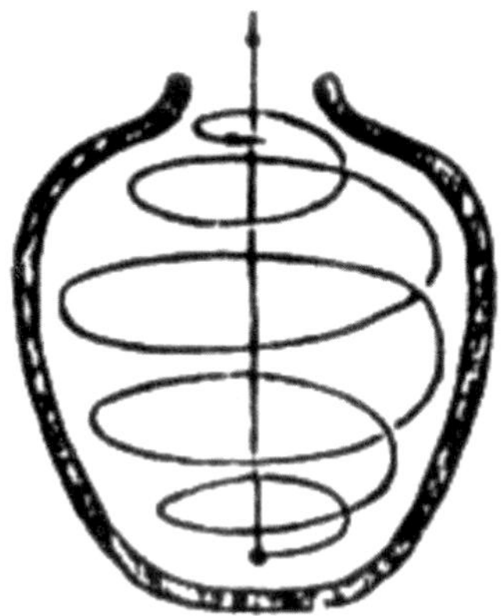

In the making of his "vessels," the basket weaver, too, uses the spiral which starts from a point and opens itself up. However, this point is brought about through the *crossing* of several reeds. We no longer have the supple lump of clay which can be formed at will. In its place we have single longer reeds which are laid over each other at right angles and held by deft fingers. Through the spirallic insertion of additional reeds, they are ultimately woven together. Prior to that the crossed reeds are bent apart in such a manner that a radiating star is formed. Basket weaving is like a precursor to weaving (cloth). One might say that the basket is a woven form in a spherical shape which is built up spirally upon the cross. The crossing of two straight lines in a right angle is a form element which offers particular strength in maintaining, binding, and fitting materials together. In this there is no longer any spherical vibration, only adamant rigidity.

Unfortunately, it is not everywhere possible to follow through and cut the reeds from the willow trees before preparing them and later soaking them long enough until they achieve the necessary suppleness for weaving. As soon as the basket is woven, the influences of the elements (here only the watery element) ceases.

Macramé also belongs here. Again, we are met by a definite point as a starting "point" for the shaping, not of a cross, but of the intertwined knots. This one begins with a spiral movement and comes to rest in crossing. Do we still remember how our children learned to knot and tie a bow in lacing up their shoes? A certain alertness is necessary. This is also necessary for arranging the knots out of which the shape of the piece of work is to come. The macramé bag, the net, and the hammock come into being more out of reflection as opposed to the pitcher, which is directly formed largely through the sensitive feeling of the hands. Old cultures, for example the Incas, used the knot to aid their memory. With the help of knot-cords events of the times were preserved, and even complete statistics were laid out. Even today, the knot in the handkerchief helps us to "bind" into our memory what wants to fly away too fast.

Still greater becomes the step which removes us from our sensing hand when it can no longer form the work itself, because the working material offers too much resistance through its hardness. Then a helper, a tool, has to be found which can take on this task and make up for the "short coming" of the hand. In metal-forming, a so-to-speak dead, mediating member moves between work-piece and hand, the chasing hammer. It becomes a fingertip which must with utmost consistency set thrust beside thrust, beginning at the center and taking up in a spirally moving form what the hand practiced in the clay—so the first little bowl can emerge out of a sheet of copper.

A climax is reached when one progresses from the forming of a cup to a covered bowl. Here an exactly fitting lid covers the top and thus encloses an inner space achieved through consistent effort. This is already the step into tenth grade, which can only be fully experienced if we think back to the plant as it unfolds spirally, full of life in the weaving light, responsive to every influence from its natural surrounding. All this lies at the basis for the sequence of forms developed by man as described above. The open space closes more and more and gains its center, its focal point, within itself.

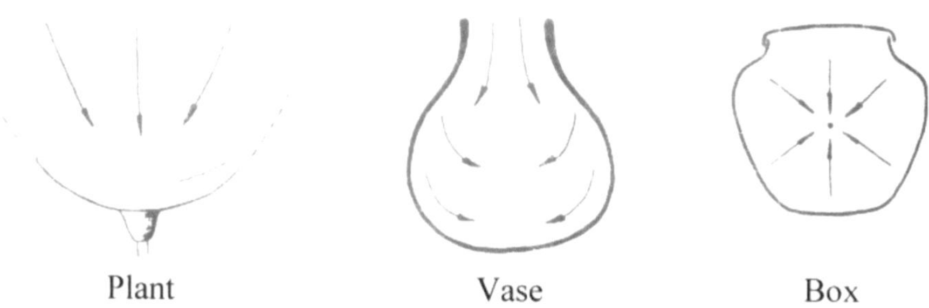

Plant Vase Box

In fact, there comes a decisive new element in grade ten through spinning. What is happening when a spiral does not develop from a point upward, but follows a suction downward from width, concentrating and contracting more and more? We know the impressive picture of the vortex which forms downward in emptying a tub. This is the forming process in making a thread, considering the old-fashioned spindle, hanging from the freely turned thread, used until the early Middle Ages everywhere.

In basket weaving we encountered already the thought of how to lengthen several shorter elements by putting them together. In spinning, this idea becomes an ingenious reality. An infinite number of short fibers are twirled into an endless thread (at least theoretically). In all this, the gravity of the earth and the heaviness of the spindle play a big role. First it was replaced by a spinning wheel, turned by hand, and later, in the sixteenth century, by the invention of the treadle wheel. The spinning wheel of today is a mechanism, and machine, which can produce completely tight, infinitely long spirals. But the human being is intimately involved with hand and foot in the whole process. Everything depends on the delicate interplay of the hands producing the wool and the foot moving the wheel, whether the thread comes out well, how thick, how fine or coarse it is spun.

Now we are not surprised that at this age (tenth grade) everything that relates to the screw is discussed. Its discovery is attributed to Archimedes (212 B.C.). He also discovered gravity and other mechanical laws. Around 200 B.C. the Greek mathematician, Apollonius of Perga, worked out the geometry of the spiral, i.e., its rigid, abstract, earthly form. The Greeks were particularly interested in the terrestrial laws. Although their world was still filled with gods, they loved life on earth so much that before their inner gaze, life after death paled into a shadow. They preferred to be a beggar on earth rather than a king in the realm of shadows.

The iron screws with which one fits things firmly together were only invented in the fifteenth century: real symbols of boring into material, of holding fast, of clamping together, and of standstill.

But this thread, which came about through solidification for the first time, gives the fundamental basis for a completely different kind of forming, namely the flat surface. In weaving, surfaces come about which today can be very wide and, again theoretically, infinitely long. How far away is all this removed from nature! In primeval times the natural "big surface" was the animal skin. What a capacity for abstraction was necessary in order to form such a surface within thin, line-like elements, brought about through right-angled intertwining! Whatever surrounds us as cloth and woven material is still based on the principle of the compact spiral and the crossing in right angles. Both these form-elements are representative of the effect of the solid and earthly.

Even today one can find with primitive peoples the precursor of the loom. These are wooden stakes rammed into the ground between which warps are extended. The first pictorial representations of looms were found in Egypt. (Middle Kingdom 2052-1785 B.C.). In both cases, the woven material comes about as a horizontal surface, lying parallel to the surface of the ground. Only later the vertical loom came about. If we imagine the globe of the earth covered with horizontal surfaces of looms, we obtain, taken altogether, the surface of a globe with its center being the center of the earth. Seen in this way, any flat surface which rests on the ground has its center in common with that of the earth and is a typical invention of the human mind, turned toward the earth.

The beauty of a cloth does not come about by the procedure of weaving alone, but through the alternation of the different colors of various threads. Weaving is purely a mechanical process, which is the first of the techniques described here that does not take place anymore in the hand of man, as spinning still does. The weaver simply makes use of that mechanism.

As long as it is a question of materials being used around man, e.g., pillows, blankets, carpets, curtains, and rugs, the original form of the rectangle, which results by necessity out of the nature of weaving, can be retained. As soon as the fabric is to be used for a human being it must take on forms adjusted to the human being. However, people who kept a natural feeling for things and happenings around them had a kind of inner reluctance to cut into the logical construction of a fabric. Therefore, the wrapping into cloth is still the custom with many peoples. The women of India put a rectangular cloth, measuring 7 x 1 m, in spiral turns around their body. The "sarong" is the dress of Indonesian women and a cloth 2 x 1 m is sown together lengthwise, and then, what is not needed of the material is stuck tightly on both sides of the body. The Malaysian word for dress means "container." Even here with us the rectangular cloth still has its significance in clothing.

But the material becomes more and more adjusted to the human form. Clothing demands that fabric be cut, regardless of its right-angled structure. Men must have experienced this as a painful process of great importance, otherwise they would not have given it the name of "tailoring" (old French: *taillour* - to cut) but perhaps "sewers or stitchers" for sewing is certainly just as important as cutting the material. While the spheric-round principle of the techniques spoken of earlier (pottery, basket weaving, and metal-forming) is used exclusively in man's surrounding, in the production of clothing man himself is the center of the piece of work. Thus, the consciousness of the youth in grade ten is led in an objective way towards the individual, and they are taken seriously even down into their own body shapes.

First, the sketch of a shirt or dress is made, and then artfully organized into single parts (pattern) which must be intelligently transferred into the piece of fabric. The purely quantitative measuring plays an important role; otherwise, in the end, the dress will not fit. The whole project will succeed only if everything has been thought through, drawn, measured properly, and the projected dress or shirt has been planned correctly from its inception. Only then can the hand begin to execute—one could almost say—thoughtlessly, the thought-through idea. Never before was the contrast between planning and execution so great; an illustration of the modern division of labor. Now the material is cut into parts and put together with the important help of the sewing machine. The agreement of correct thinking and skilled execution has the happy result of a work well done.

With carpentry and cabinet making the turn from nature to abstract thinking is even more noticeable. Up to grade eight the children acquainted themselves with wood through carving wood as it comes from the garden or forest, as trunks with bark and branches, hewn into coarse pieces. None of these pieces lies with an even surface on the workbench. The roundness of the trunk, the spiral growth, the aliveness of the grain are touchable for eye and hand.

Only in grade ten, in cabinet-making, is the board truly experienced. The flat surface has to be worked in right angles for boxes and shelves, and horizontally for a stool. The effort in all this is to exclude, as completely as possible, the living characteristic qualities of the wood, so to speak, to outwit the wood. Such a trick is employed, for example, in the keeper of a table top; this is to prevent its warping, which would remind us of its origin and become round again as it once was, in its live structure. This cannot be allowed anymore and is prevented by the keeper. What was previously round is now criticized as crooked and dismissed as faulty. Only a certain way of "working" the wood is accepted, because nothing can be undone anymore (note the swelling and contraction of the board, especially across its width, with which it partakes in the humidity of the surrounding air). We know this well from our drawers and doors in so far as they are still made out of wood. Who is not annoyed during the humid season when they stick? We do not like to be reminded in such a way of the original aliveness of the wood.

Stimulated by the flat surfaces of the wood, new needs arose, namely to widen the natural size of a board sawed out of a tree trunk. This became possible through planing, joining, and gluing. Who is able to still see in a glued wooden plate the origin whence it came, the tree trunk? Let's look once carefully at a sheet of plywood; out of the thin wooden surfaces, shaved from the trunk, which are always laid in right angles over each other, there came about (in theory only) an endless flat surface, from which all the living, natural breathing of the wood has been removed. Here all life-processes have been locked out. The operation to produce a piece of carpentry is not different from the work order of a dress in tailoring. Thus, here also, the conception, the thought must precede the blueprint of the project. Exact control, the knowledge of a variety of specialized tools, under certain circumstances, the help of machines, which on account of their danger may not be used by pupils, are necessary. Do we find here still any process of work which can be executed without a tool, with the hands alone?

We can see how tailoring and carpentry have many common fundamental features, while at the same time they are very specialized in their character. In carpentry, for example, the right angle—quite apart from the question of shape—is predominant, while in tailoring, man himself is absolutely the "yardstick" in the truest sense of the word.

Have we perhaps also noticed that all these handwork blocks are dealing in principle with the forming of sheaths of various kinds and purposes? Even the caring for the food which we see growing in the garden serves the maintenance of our body, which in the end, is a sheath or vessel for the individual soul-spiritual being of man.

Let us return to carpentry once more and imagine a chest, a typical cabinet. We shrink it down to a length and width of 2 x 1 handbreadths. We are able to produce this little "cabinet" out of cardboard and use it for storing letters. We come to the making of cardboard boxes in grade eleven, and this leads on directly into bookbinding. Now we have "sheaths" for the written and printed word. Thus, also, the spiritual creativity of a person is integrated into the general theme of the handwork canon.

Rudolf Steiner also wanted the manufacturing of paper to be taught in grade eleven. The invention of paper is lost in the twilight of early pre-Christian centuries. The first paper-mill in Germany was established in Nuremberg by Ulmann Stromer in 1390. Although paper goes back to very old times, it is for us a modern work material. However, paper is fundamentally different from any fabric, even if it is as thin as a film. The short fibers of paper are indiscriminately mixed in a watery solution (the more chaotic the solution the better) because in scooping off the fibers with a sieve and then as the water drips off, the solution mats together, which makes the paper firmer.

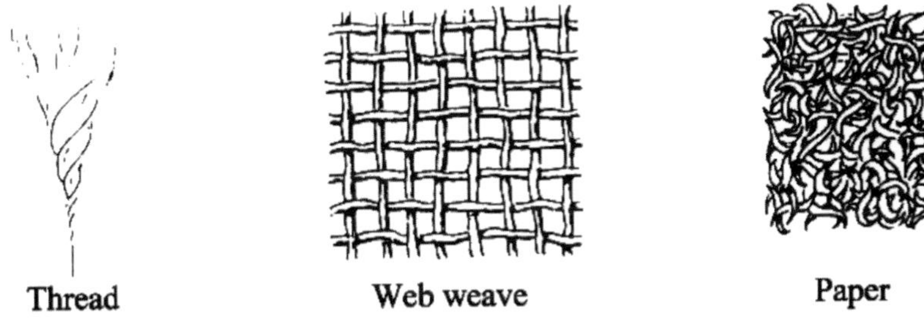

Thread **Web weave** **Paper**

Out of this "atomization" comes a material the origin of which one does not recognize anymore. One can almost speak of a "synthetic material" which has found a great number of modern imitations, e.g., masonite, particle board, and homesote—all are made out of crushed or broken up pieces, held together with a binding agent.

Some aspects of what has been described in this article have not yet been realized in a satisfactory way; but with the insight and help of all parents and teachers, we shall continue to work further on the task given to us.

---

*This edited article was translated by Rudolf Copple and is included with permission of Michael Martin. If you are able to read German, you should read his wonderful book, ***Der künsterisch-handwerkliche Unterricht in der Waldorfschule***, ISBN #3-7725-0254-7, published by Freies Geistesleben, 1991.

23

Re-imagining Handwork and the Practical Arts

Impulses for Educating the Modern Human Being

by

Aonghus Gordon

During the last two decades Waldorf pupils have found themselves in a growing dilemma. Embedded within their consciousness is a potential capacity to resolve considerable practical and environmental problems through the interdisciplinary approach to their learning, but their ability to manifest this increasingly requires an as yet undeveloped context. We must present our Waldorf students with more practical challenges and environmental issues, because such issues alone offer the pupil the chance to unite all aspects of Waldorf education harmoniously in their thinking, feeling, and willing. The solving of practical problems lifts the will toward a deeper social, ethical morality. Environmental problems are moral problems requiring people to offer solutions out of creative, practical experience.

Waldorf teachers are called upon to intensify and reappraise craft, handwork, and technology in schools. One of the principle tenets of the Waldorf approach is that thinking arises out of activity and movement in the early developmental stages of the child.

The philosopher Emmanuel Kant said, "The hand is the outer brain of the human being!" This creates a powerful image for all handwork and craft teachers, an image that needs to be taken more seriously in view of the accelerating decline in opportunities to move actively and appropriately in early childhood.

First, We Need to Redesign the School's Grounds

A craft curriculum accessing the primary processes and substances of the environment can engender a quality of integrity, particularly for the adolescent. This orientation is entirely dependent on a new awareness of the school grounds and the landscape at large. Biodynamic principles can play a key role in supporting the educational process and help to make the "outdoor classroom" more inviting.

Creating educational intimacy within the outdoor classroom and perceiving the learning process are the challenge. This challenge is ignored at our peril, as the intellect of the adolescent increasingly searches for evidence of an imprint on or mastery of the practical world. If the will is not lifted up through creative practical activity and training, it works as an instinctual drive. Creative problem solving through practical work servicing human needs is also the first step toward discovering "social empathy." Brought up into consciousness through contemporary ideas of sustainability, it potentially allows the adolescent to encounter a new social ethic.

Goethe required any serious student who wished to understand the environment in which he or she participated to become conversant with the *genius loci*, the spirit of the place. The size of the school grounds is no impediment to this process of reengaging with the land. Budgets have already been created for the upkeep of the land; all that is needed is a new consciousness which makes the land and what issues from it part of the educational experience.

Schools that have researched and entered into this relationship have found a new route of identity and, more importantly, reincorporated the craft skills of the landscape into the craft curriculum of the school. A survey over the course of one year in which all aspects of the school's grounds and landscape are touched on by each class in the school brings new ownership and awareness. The gardening curriculum finds a new context the identification, enhancement, or creation of a water area demonstrates pride of place in the development and the diversification that is required to reenliven the etheric sheath of the school. Plants and hedges can be pruned and used as a source for making Easter nests in the kindergarten, for basketry or chair caning in the high school, and for providing coppicing or charcoal for use in a primitive forge. Clay pits can be dug to build a bread oven or to create pottery. Over the year an emerging alchemy of the four elements will become apparent from the school grounds as each becomes a sacred place.

New skills and teaching methods are required to take children to new experiential frontiers. These frontiers enable imaginative pictures to take effect, and powerful feelings of empathy for the environment and new exercises in the will to emerge. In schools where this process of developing the landscape is taking on an educational imprint, the context becomes child centered, not recreational, not economic, but applied through educational practice and supported by biodynamic principles. The school thereby takes ownership of, and responsibility for, the immediate landscape, which becomes increasingly transparent to the pupils, particularly as they ascend toward the upper school and the dawning of their intellectual capacities. Morality toward the earth is engendered.

As the pupil ascends in age with new-found intellectual skills, craftwork is gradually replaced by a crafted landscape organism in which sustainable environmental practice is underpinned by an ethic of sustainability but enacted through the freewill gesture of the pupil. The pupil moves from "point to periphery." The building of a water cleansing reed bed system, a practical ecology in working with the kingdoms of nature and the elements, to service the growing environmental degradation, offers the older pupils the opportunity for self-judgment. Their highly developed intellectual capacities can be channeled into servicing environmental and human requirements. This may be called a new form of living technology. In this way aspects of the upper school science curriculum can externalize from the laboratory into the environment and have direct application. One may be even so bold as to call it a new form of practical literacy.

During a twelfth grade project in which pupils were placed into an environment in which they had to resource materials and processes to sustain themselves, the pupils encountered a high level of motivation and skill in resolving their requirements: building a baker's oven to cook food, constructing a compost toilet to deal with their personal waste, creating tools and implements. Their level of engagement and exercised "problem-solving skills" is testified through the following series of impressions by two students:

Working with the issue of sustainability in mind we acquired hands-on experience of the use of such materials as wood, clay and iron in our activities. The result was that each of the four groups faced its own individual challenges, which the students themselves had to overcome with guidance from the tutors where necessary. Thus, the complexities of a sewage system, a bread oven and how to fit a chair together without straight pieces of wood were tackled and overcome.

– Saul Grant

We soon discovered that the activities were not dissimilar to arts and craft lessons . . . but with one significant difference: rather than simply watching and the taking part in a craft, which, it seems, is productive only insofar as it provides gifts for one's relatives . . . we were actually applying what we learned to serve a useful human need. Building a compost toilet requires much physical labor . . . the idea behind the compost toilet being that, by giving back what we take from the soil, we refrain from disrupting the natural cycle, and simultaneously develop an awareness of being responsible for our own wastage rather than flushing it away and forgetting about it. This pleasing balance of intellectual and practical learning generated a real enthusiasm amongst us . . .self sufficiency in a facility devoid field meant that each group became dependent on the other for resources. We were able to develop a consciousness of some of the most pertinent environmental issues today, by way of direct application.

– Danielle Radojcin

Eighteen-year-olds today will often be found searching through an intellectual framework to test the evidence and correctness of their thoughts and actions placed within the contemporary context of sustainability. These pupils were thirsty to have themselves tested, not solely on an intellectual level, but so as to confront a threshold experience of an inner nature, a test which sustains and contributes long term to human development. What the Hiram Trust offered the pupils is no different in essence from that which is fostered by the Steiner/Waldorf pedagogical framework.

Through such activities a school can develop a new and potent resource and an educational framework that incorporates the outdoor classroom as a complement to the existing learning environment.

The Problems Faced by Modern Adolescents

Today, increasingly, teachers observe restlessness, hyperactivity, and above all concentration difficulties as well as a dislocation between point and periphery in the child's growing awareness. If unchecked in adolescence, three powerful subcultures are likely to take effect. The intellect that is not incorporated into the world of imagination becomes conceited and arrogant, while the search for the imagination will frequently lead to drug taking. If the will is not diverted into appropriate skillful activity and endeavor, it will commonly become criminalized and search for extreme experiences, such as joy riding, to compensate for the absence of movement and activity. And if the feeling life of the adolescent is aberrant, where feelings of devotion are not cultivated, an overt form of sexualized behavior often arises. These three counter pictures often ensnare the adolescent. Practical skillful craftwork within itself has the opportunity of reembodying thinking, feeling, and willing—in thinking, the preplanning of the conceptual framework; in feeling, the sense of purpose in the service of a social context; and in willing, the capacity to fashion and execute the form. However, it is becoming increasingly apparent that all this may still not be sufficient. The environmental context, as yet an undiscovered emerging parameter for the later and more mature development of adolescence, offers many challenges to enact a new ethic based around the principles of sustainability, a new craftsmanship of the environment, a living technology.

As a result of fundamental questions, both from parents and teachers, as to the future direction of Waldorf education, particularly regarding practical skills and an understanding of a cohesive approach to the curriculum as a whole, the Hiram Trust has developed what we might call the concept of the intelligent hand. The emphasis of the Trust is to incorporate "point and periphery" as regards the classroom and the environment of the school through the work of the hand, for it is clear to all concerned that craftwork is embedded in the development of human consciousness and has a history of 10,000 years. This history is additionally embedded in the Steiner/Waldorf school, in particular in the main lesson curriculum, and can be sourced as a further opportunity of extending the range of practical skills that enable the experience of learning to be grounded though the context of the material and the intended purpose of the objects made. Sourcing the materials is essential to enable children to handle at first hand the three kingdoms of nature and engage in the four elements.

Reenlivening the Sense of Movement

The remarkable aspect of movement inherent in executing primary craft activities, whether rolling felt or shaping hot metal, is the preordained nature of the movement itself. The movement arcs that are inscribed on the material, and developed by the pupil, resonate in the etheric body of the child as a "cosmic imprint." True agility of movement in craftsmanship, when inscribed on paper, even remind one of the movements of the planetary spheres. Few movement activities are so objective, as the craft movement is defined by the laws inherent in the quality of the material and the purpose of the object. Egotistical movement is limited, if the object being undertaken serves a human social world, such as a knife from the iron age forge, a chair from green woodwork, slippers from felt.

Reanimating movement in the child and adolescent serves to release the etheric body out of the muscular structure, which is so often frozen, even in a state of shock. Releasing the fluidity of movement through a craft activity may be described as accessing a slipstream of movement in which the pupil or adolescent is held.

The child's first movements, gripping, rotating, sliding, lifting, crawling, or, more simply put, exploring the three dimensions of space, are available in different measures of intensity in the simple craft activities drawn out of a primary craft curriculum and can be used as a recapitulation of missed stages of development, an increasingly common phenomenon. Just as children's early drawings contain primordial shapes and movements, these movements are primordial and are a prerequisite to achieving a healthy integrated relationship to the world. Where a movement experience becomes rhythmical, out of which a skill develops, there is a term often used to describe it: "I can do it in my sleep." In observing this state of awareness, something interesting happens. It is as if this awareness comes out of the stream of time. The skill is gained through past experience, but it brings something toward the individual out of the future. It is possible to experience non-time, in other words, a state of presence in which opportunities arise so as to observe oneself in movement. This is a profoundly therapeutic experience, and many pupils touch this point when they become more skillful in their movement articulation. This "presence" can be described as a state of self-healing, as it can act as a path toward self-knowledge.

Curriculum for a Waldorf High School

The following diagram offers a coherent approach to the integration of craft project work related to the environment and landscape. Its age-appropriateness is dependent on a comprehensive and flexible understanding of child development. The child's descent into matter starts with the tactile experience of wool at the kindergarten stage, continuing through to the fashioning of useful objects in clay and metal that are transformed through the control of fire. Engaging in a craft activity appropriate to the stage of development reached by the child and adolescent facilitates the descent into, and subsequent transformation of, matter.

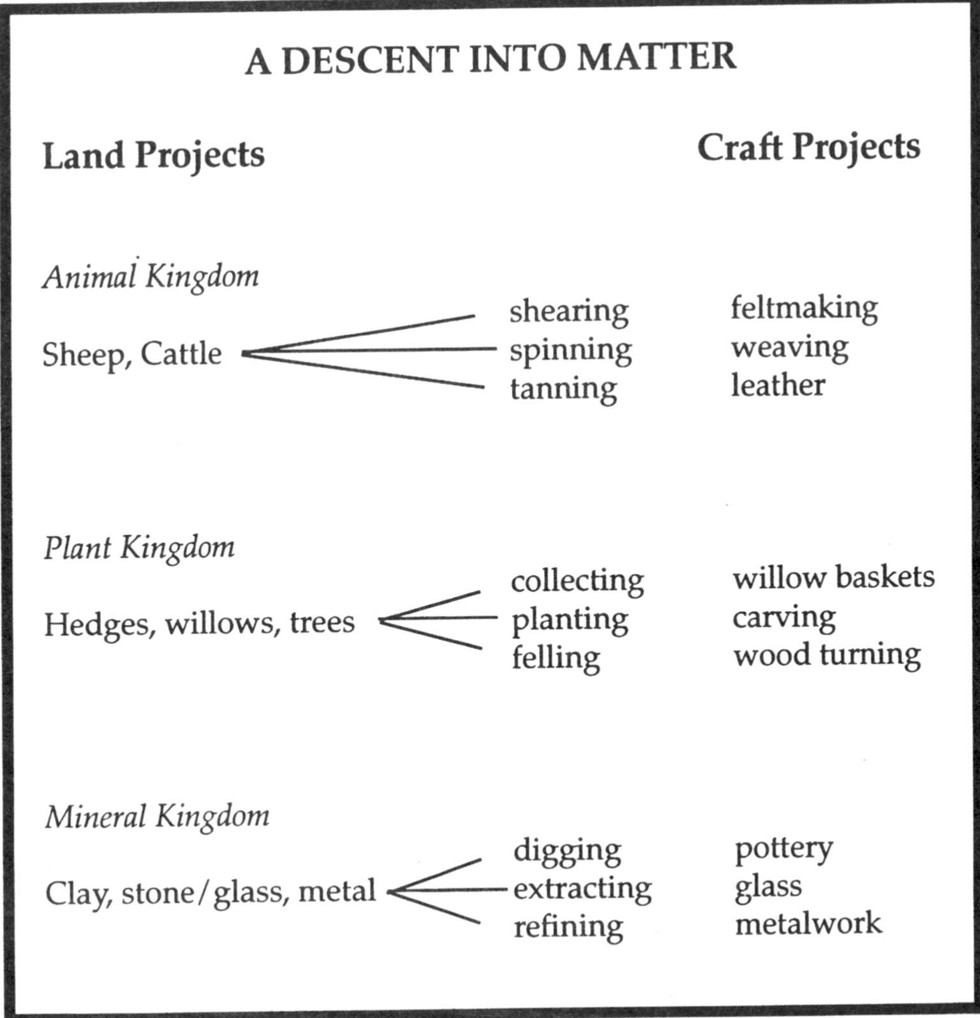

Activities promoted by the Hiram Trust can be organized in an open and flexible framework around the theme of "a descent into matter." This descent follows the incarnation path of the child into adolescence and uses the age-appropriate practical skill to engage the path of incarnation.

The nine ancient crafts of mankind, sourced from the three kingdoms of nature and found at the interface of the four elements, arise from within the inspiration of the Steiner/Waldorf curriculum. By sourcing the primary materials, as is so often done in the kindergarten, we are in effect starting to reinvigorate the child's sensory perception of the world through the hand.

The age-appropriateness of any activity must arise out of a clear understanding of child development in conjunction with the teacher's observation. With the advent of current lifestyles teachers are finding that a more fundamental and therapeutic intensification in gestures of movement is increasingly required to cultivate healthy development and limb, hand, and eye coordination. Fewer children cook, climb trees, play on farms and in forests. The natural world is more and more a foreign experience. The world of play requires an intensification and orientation toward the practical.

This practical aspect is more consciously applied to the main lesson curriculum in the third grade with the awakening to landscape, shelter and buildings. Foundations are laid during this period for the craft curriculum to work on later in the development of thinking skills.

By employing empathetic processes and materials at source, appropriate access is granted to what has often been seen as premature experience in the past in developing a handcraft curriculum for the younger children in the school. For example, with regard to blacksmithing, Rudolf Steiner requested that the blacksmith work back to back with the kindergarten, so the rhythm, fire, and stature of the blacksmith imprints itself on the senses of the child. But blacksmithing itself is only practiced in the tenth grade. Perceiving the elements of blacksmithing as opposed to executing a functional item enables children in their fourth grade main lesson on Norse mythology to become Thor at the anvil in the blacksmith workshop, guided by the element of fire and the rhythm of beating.

A child in kindergarten bending and twisting sticks into shapes and sharpening them on rocks is exploring the first qualities of resistance. Incorporating the activity of whittling as the first part of an elementary school's woodwork curriculum is of particular value so as to give the foundations of coordination prior to the more sophisticated expectations of judgment in cutting and carving.

Looking at the textiles curriculum in a similar way, the kindergarten children on a walk will collect wool from the hedges and hawthorn.

This point of contact is a treasured moment for the children as they experience the soft, delicate, warm, and ephemeral quality of the material. The children will invariably return with their pockets full and will compress and form the raw wool into nests, figures, animals, or a simple wall hanging. This is in fact the start of the textile curriculum. Its emergence and appropriate application will be based on the judgment of the teacher.

In ***The Study of Man*** Rudolf Steiner left the craft teachers with a remarkable opportunity of fashioning their curriculum based largely upon their own observation of the children, their perception and understanding. This meeting of the material from the kingdoms of the earth and the school teacher's understanding of child development is a creative area in the Steiner/Waldorf approach, leaving a free space for development and research as regards curriculum content.

In looking at a broader application of craft and practical skills activities in the lower part of the school, inspiration can be drawn from the earliest human craft activities. An interesting guideline for the application of a particular craft activity is to observe the gesture in the activity and the density of the material required. The denser the material the more appropriate the activity becomes for the development of the adolescent.

Encountering the resistance of the material encourages forces of self-judgment and a pragmatic testing of the boundaries of the materials. It is notable that leather work, wood turning, and metalwork in particular offer the highest levels of resistance in material, whereas papermaking, felt and clay work harmonize more readily with the lower school curriculum. Negotiating fire is a crucial ingredient in the upper school experience, as its potentially destructive forces need to be controlled, understood, and directed. Activities such as casting metal, where the adolescent prejudges, thinks, and makes a model, require an attitude of complete responsibility for the perfection or imperfection of the crafted item. In the repetition of the item all flaws are revealed. Craft activities that necessitate a high degree of judgment and intellectual rigor support the pupil in the last years of schooling. Challenging the adolescent to place the activity in a sustainable and environmental context, where rigor, reflection, and prejudgment are required at each step, directs him or her into new areas of application and toward a new ethic of deed.

AFTERWORD

The Hiram Trust and Ruskin Mill

The Hiram Trust is an educational initiative that was set up in Great Britain in 1994. It was inspired by similar work in Holland which was established to deepen the understanding of the practical skills curriculum in Waldorf schools. This was in response to the increasing tendency towards abstraction in the learning environment that has taken place over the last thirty years.

Inspired by the "Arts and Crafts Movement," this contemporary craft education provided by the Ruskin Mill Further Education Centre in Nailsworth, Gloucester, and the Life Science Trust in Scotland, which promotes Goethean science, aims to promote experiential learning by encouraging and developing activity in the "outdoor classroom." This requires a renewal of the craft and associated practical arts curriculum related to the environment. This approach fosters the ethos of education for sustainability.

Ruskin Mill was built for the manufacture of woolen cloth during the 1820s. It served as the home for a number of other artisan industries, including the manufacture of shoes and turned brassware and the production of aniline dye, before falling into disrepair. Fresh life came to the Mill in the 1960s when it became both a family home and a small conference center dedicated to working with the insights of John Ruskin, William Morris, and Rudolf Steiner. A number of craft people were attracted to the Mill, and in the 1980s the systematic redevelopment of the building began in earnest together with the formation of some independent craft workshops.

Around this time young people from a nearby special school were invited to take an active part in rebuilding the original water wheel. It was their enthusiasm for this task and also the interest they showed in the work of the craft people and their workshops that triggered the beginning of the Ruskin Mill Further Education Centre.

Working alongside craftsmen and women passionate about their craft and keen to share their enthusiasm became an integral part of the Centre's focus, enabling many young people to enjoy the stimulation of creating beautiful and practical articles to a quality beyond their expectations. They experienced a new outlook on life and found within themselves new self-confidence.

Using the school grounds and an adjacent woodland, a full range of craft activities was developed, including green woodwork, charcoal production, forging in an Iron Age forge, clay digging and pottery, blacksmithing, papermaking, leather processing, gardening, farming, forest management, textiles, stained glass, metal casting, and woodworking. Added to these were associated activities such as house construction, auto mechanics, photography, music, art, performing arts, and technology. The activities became the central teacher for these adolescents. However, they wrote essays, did mathematics, read, computed, and did other "normal" school activities in connection with their practical work.

For further information, please write to Ruskin Mill Education Centre, Old Bristol Road, Nailsworth, Gloucestershire GL60LA, England.

24

Conclusion

by

David Mitchell

The principal good of education is to create men who are capable of doing new things, not simply of repeating what other generations have done.
- Jean Piaget

Recent neurological research has confirmed that mobility and dexterity in the fine motor muscles, especially the hand, stimulate cellular development in the brain, and so strengthen the physical instrument of thinking. The intention of the authors of this book is both to support this observation and to show the reader, through an outline of the handwork and practical arts curriculum, how fortunate children are who have found their way to Waldorf education.

Many forms of thinking (analytical, synthetic, teleological, causal, and so forth) need to be learned in today's complex society. It is our task as teachers to apply these various ways of thinking to the subject matter we are teaching. In nurturing the cognitive development of their students, Waldorf schools aim to include training in judgment, in the sense of discretion—through handwork and practical arts.

The capacity for conceptual thought lies on a higher level of cognitive development. The process of abstraction can be exercised by having students analyze their own work. The method of examining why a piece of copper became too thin in a particular area, or why a joint of a compound dovetail didn't fit, lends itself to such mental evaluation. Self-observation, self-evaluation, and the capacity to take on responsibility are characteristics of personal growth.

Skills learned in the crafts become the development of practical consciousness. This practical consciousness has its genesis in an increased power of observation. The training of the power of perception is extended in the upper grades to precise observation.

The task of the teacher today is not to structure the minds of the students, but rather to enable them to grow to new dimensions—dimensions that may even exceed our own understanding. In such a manner the teacher of the present can serve the future. Teaching must become a continuous learning process for the teacher as well as for the student.

Educators can learn a lesson from examining industry. The 3M Company went from producing sandpaper to roofing shingles, to scotch tape, to magnetic tape, to photocopying, and then to reflective signs. All of these products require a common skill—how to apply a closely controlled layer of material on a flexible base. The kind of creative thinking that evolved new products at 3M can be stimulated by a proper relationship between thinking and will activities in high school. Such creative thinking helps people to avoid setting self-imposed boundaries that cut off their vision and their reach.

By the time a student graduates from high school, he or she should have made a connection with the main technologies of our age, from the computer, to an understanding of the internal combustion engine, to an understanding of what happens when we flip a switch and a light shines. It is necessary to understand these things in order to feel at home in the world.

Handwork and the practical arts in fact address the critical problem for young people of how to feel secure in the modern world. These hands-on subjects do so not only by developing thinking and will—but also by engendering love: love of self (self-esteem, through accomplishment), love for others (through social interaction and learning new capacities for giving), love of the joy of creative work, love of artistry, and love of ongoing self-development. Handwork and the practical arts refine and nurture the capacity for love by strengthening and harmonizing the rhythmic system of the body—the heart and circulation plus the lungs and breathing. The greatest creative force is love, and love's enthusiasm and joy typically suffuse a handwork classroom or practical arts studio. That attitude, carried into life, combined with the realistic sense of self-worth that these lessons have cultivated, are attributes essential to achieving success in any endeavor—especially to finding one's place in the world.

No individual will be able to retain his or her independence in our contemporary working world unless an emancipatory education has endowed that person with the practical capacity to do so. Practical subjects, artistic lessons, and activities involving the hand can no longer be seen merely as supportive and enlivening factors of the curriculum. Rather they are absolutely necessary in the education of our youth, who face a complex and changing world.

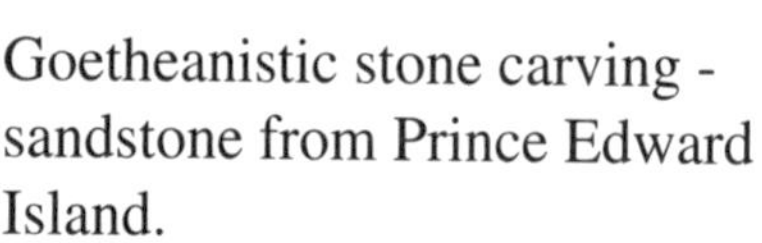

Goetheanistic stone carving - sandstone from Prince Edward Island.